London Gardens

A Seasonal Guide

London
Gardens

A Seasonal Guide

with *28 colour illustrations*

LORNA PARKER

First published in 2001 by Lorna Lister

This revised and updated edition published in 2004 by
Watling St Publishing
The Glen
Southrop
Lechlade
Gloucestershire
GL7 3NY

Printed in Singapore

Copyright © Lorna Parker 2004

ISBN 1-904153-18-6

24681097531

Contents

Introduction

London contains a myriad of green spaces which are in turn filled with a kaleidoscope of plants, all displaying a pattern of continually changing colours, forms and textures. In our daily lives, bustling about, we often fail to notice or appreciate the spectacular free show that nature gives us even in the heart of one of the largest urban environments on earth. However if you do feel you can spare the time to visit some of London's most remarkable floral displays, this book will help. For each month it sets out the plants in flower and the horticultural features, in season. It then lists the gardens where these plants or features are considered worth visiting. The main section of the book contains all the aforementioned gardens with a colourful personal description accompanied by concise, practical visitor information.

Both well and lesser-known gardens, such as some roof gardens, wild flower gardens and several private gardens which open under the National Gardens Scheme on few days each year, are included. All the featured gardens lie within the Greater London area and can be reached on London Transport, the nearest bus routes and underground or overground train stations are given.

In addition to over 70 individual gardens, the book contains some of 'The Great Trees of London' which are specific trees so designated by 'Trees for London' due to their great age, size, remarkable shape or historical or cultural associations. These may be interesting to see at any time of year, although some species are especially attractive in spring and autumn. It also includes the Marie Curie Foundation's 'Fields of Hope' which are large fields of daffodils planted in very visible and public sites as part of the Charity's campaign to raise awareness of cancer care. The fields give a dazzling display of yellow when they flower each March or April.

Whether you want to visit large scale botanical spectacles brimming with colour and fragrance, find peace among a woodland or hidden wild flower meadow or take the family to tackle a maze on a frosty winter's day, this book will suggest clearly what to see, where to go and when. It will be of great use to those who enjoy discovering new gardens or just relaxing among the joys of nature.

List of Gardens

Avenue House Arboretum

Avery Hill Park

Barbican Conservatory

Battersea Park

Brockwell Park

Burgh House

Camley Street Nature Park

Cannizaro Park

Capel Manor Gardens

Carlyle's House Garden

Chelsea Physic Garden

Chiswick House Gardens

Choumert Square Garden

Chumleigh Multicultural Gardens

Columbia Road Flower Market

Crystal Palace Park

Dulwich Park

East Ham Nature Reserve

Eltham Palace Gardens

Emslie Horniman Pleasance Park

Fenton House Gardens

Fulham Palace Gardens

Geffrye Museum Gardens

Golders Green Crematorium

Golders Hill Park

Gray's Inn Gardens

Great Trees of London

Greenwich Royal Park

Gunnersbury Park

Ham House

Hampton Court Palace

Hill Garden

Holland Park

Horniman Museum Gardens

Hyde Park

Kensal Green Cemetery

Kensington Gardens

Kensington Roof Gardens

Kenwood House Gardens

Lady Venice's Garden

Lambeth Community Centre Garden (NGS)

Lambeth Palace Garden (NGS)

Lincoln's Inn Fields

London Wildlife Garden Centre

London Wildlife Trust Nature
Reserves

Marble Hill Park

Marie Curie Cancer Care
Fields of Hope

Middle Temple Gardens

Mile End Park

Morden Hall Park

Museum of Garden History
Garden

Museum of London's Nursery
Garden

Myddelton House Gardens

Natural History Museum Wildlife
Garden

17a Navarino Gardens (NGS)

Number 1 Poultry Roof Garden

Nunhead Cemetery

Osterley Park

Peckham Rye Park

Postman's Park

Queen's Park

Ravenscourt Park

Regent's Park

Richmond Park

Rookery Gardens

Roots & Shoots

Royal Botanic Gardens
(Kew Gardens)

Royal Hospital Gardens
(Ranelagh Gardens)

Royal Institute of British
Architects Garden

St James's Park

St John's Wood Church Burial
Ground

St Michael's Convent Garden
(NGS)

Syon Park

Thames Barrier Park

Tibetan Peace Garden (Samten
Kyil)

Trent Country Park

Trinity Hospice Garden (NGS)

Victoria and Albert Museum
Garden

Victoria Park

The Watergardens (NGS)

Waterlow Park

West Ham Park

Westminster Abbey Garden

Monthly Lists

With recommended Gardens for visiting

January and February

Flowers

Christmas Roses (Helleborus spp) : *Myddelton House; Royal Botanic Gardens (Order Beds)*

Coloured Willows (Salix spp) : *Holland Park; Hyde Park (The Dell); Royal Botanic Gardens (Secluded Garden)*

Hollies (Ilex spp) : *Capel Manor; Hampton Court Palace; Kensal Green Cemetery; Kensington Gardens; Osterley Park; Royal Botanic Gardens (by Temperate House); West Ham Park*

Snowdrops (Galanthus spp) : *Cannizaro Park; Chelsea Physic Garden; Eltham Palace; Myddelton House; West Ham Park*

Winter-flowering Heathers (Erica spp) : *Cannizaro Park; Holland Park; Richmond Park (Isabella Plantation); Royal Botanic Gardens (by Pagoda); St John's Wood Church; West Ham Park*

Witch Hazels (Hamamelis spp) : *Hyde Park (The Dell); Richmond Park (Isabella Plantation); Royal Botanic Gardens (King William's Temple)*

Items of Special Interest

Alpine Houses : *Capel Manor; Royal Botanic Gardens*

Container Gardens : *Capel Manor; Lady Venice; London Wildlife Garden Centre*

Interesting Tree Profiles : *Great Trees of London*; Avenue House Arboretum*

Japanese Gardens : *Battersea Park; Capel Manor; Holland Park; Royal Botanic Gardens*

Knot Gardens, Parterres & Topiary:

Knot Gardens *Capel Manor; Fulham Palace; Hampton Court Palace; Museum of Garden History*

Parterres *Ham House; Hampton Court Palace; Royal Botanic Gardens*

Topiary *Capel Manor; Ham House; Syon Park; Thames Barrier Park*

Mazes : *Capel Manor; Crystal Palace Park; Hampton Court Palace*

Peace Gardens : *Tibetan Peace Garden*

Roof Gardens : *Kensington Roof Garden; No. 1 Poultry; Royal Institute of British Architects*

Tropical Conservatories : *Avery Hill; Barbican; Capel Manor; Royal Botanic Gardens; Myddelton House; Syon Park*

*Great Trees in London registered as 'special' due to their great age, size, extraordinary shape, cultural or historical significance or particular importance to wildlife.

The location for 6 of these is listed in the section for 'Great Trees of London' in the main part of the book.

March

Flowers

Camellias (Camellia spp) [early flowering species] : *Chiswick House; Hampton Court Palace; Holland Park; Kensington Gardens; Richmond Park; Royal Botanic Gardens*

Crocuses (Crocus spp) : *Cannizaro Park; Golders Green Crematorium; Hampton Court Palace; Myddelton House; Royal Botanic Gardens*

Daffodils (Narcissus spp) : *Cannizaro Park; Eltham Palace; Golders Green Crematorium; Gunnersbury Park; Hampton Court Palace; Lambeth Palace (NGS*); Marie Curie Cancer Care 'Fields of Hope'***; Myddelton House; Osterley Park; Trent Country Park; Westminster Abbey Garden*

Orchids [indoor Orchid festival] : *Royal Botanic Gardens*

Primroses (Primula spp) : *Hampton Court Palace; London Wildlife Trust Garden Centre; Museum of Garden History; Trinity Hospice (NGS*)*

Rhododendrons (Rhododendron spp) [early flowering species] : *Cannizaro Park; Chiswick House; Crystal Palace Park; Dulwich Park, Golders Green Crematorium; Golders Hill Park; Greenwich Park; Hill Garden; Holland Park; Kensington Gardens; Kenwood House; Osterley Park; Richmond Park; Royal Botanic Gardens; Syon Park; Waterlow Park*

Items of Special Interest

Interesting Tree Profiles : *Great Trees of London**; Avenue House Arboretum*

Japanese Gardens : *Battersea Park; Capel Manor; Holland Park; Royal Botanic Gardens*

Roof Gardens : *Kensington Roof Garden; No. 1 Poultry; Royal Institute of British Architects*

Spring Bedding : *Cannizaro Park; Chiswick House; Golders Hill Park; Greenwich Park; Hampton Court Palace; Holland Park; Horniman Museum; Hyde Park; Kensington Gardens; Lincoln's Inn Fields; Myddelton House; Queen's Park; Regent's Park; Richmond Park; Royal Botanic Gardens; Rookery Gardens; St James's Park; St John's Wood Church; Victoria Park; West Ham Park*

Spring Bulbs : *Brockwell Park; Capel Manor; Carlyle's House; Fenton House; Golders Green Crematorium; Greenwich Park; Horniman Museum Gardens; Lambeth Palace (NGS*); Museum of Garden History; Myddelton House; Roots & Shoots; Royal Botanic Gardens; Trinity Hospice (NGS*)*

Topiary Gardens : *Capel Manor; Ham House; Hampton Court Palace; Museum of Garden History; Syon Park*

Tropical Conservatories : *Avery Hill; Barbican; Capel Manor; Royal Botanic Gardens; Myddelton House; Syon Park*

Wild Flowers : *Capel Manor; Camley Nature Park; Dulwich Park; East Ham Nature Reserve; Holland Park; Kenwood House; London Wildlife Trust Garden Centre; Morden Hall Park; Natural History Museum Wildlife Garden; Nunhead Cemetery; Peckham Rye Park; Roots & Shoots; Syon Park; Thames Barrier Park*

Woodland Gardens : *Capel Manor; Holland Park; Kenwood House; Lambeth Palace (NGS*); Morden Hall Park; Nunhead Cemetery; Royal Botanic Gardens; Syon Park*

*Private gardens opening on certain days under the National Gardens Scheme (NGS), see page 30.

**Great Trees in London registered as 'special' due to either their age, size, extraordinary shape, cultural or historical significance or particular importance to wildlife. The location for six of these is listed in 'Great Trees of London' in the main part of the book.

***Fields of daffodils planted by the Marie Curie Cancer Care Charity to raise awareness of the needs of cancer patients. Locations of the sites in and around London are listed in the section for Marie Curie Cancer Care 'Fields of Hope' in the main part of the book.

April

Flowers

Bluebells (Hyacinthoides non-scripta) : *Kenwood House; Nunhead Cemetery; Osterley Park; Richmond Park; Royal Botanic Gardens; St John's Wood Church; Victoria Park*

Camellias (Camellia spp) : *Chiswick House; Hampton Court Palace; Holland Park; Kensington Gardens; Osterley Park; Richmond Park; Royal Botanic Gardens*

Cherry Blossom (Prunus spp) : *Brockwell Park; Carlyle's House; Crystal Palace Park; Fulham Palace; Golders Hill Park; Gray's Inn Gardens; Hampton Court Palace; Kensington Gardens; Lincoln's Inn Fields; Middle Temple Gardens; Osterley Park; Ravenscourt Park; Royal Botanic Gardens; St James's Park; St John's Wood Church; Syon Park; Tibetan Peace Garden; Trinity Hospice (NGS*); Victoria Park; West Ham Park; Westminster Abbey Garden*

Daffodils (Narcissus spp) : *Cannizaro Park; Eltham Palace; Golders Green Crematorium; Gunnersbury Park; Hampton Court Palace; Lambeth Palace (NGS*); Marie Curie Cancer Care 'Fields of Hope'**; Myddelton House; Osterley Park; Trent Country Park; Westminster Abbey Garden*

Magnolias (Magnolia spp) : *Cannizaro Park; Capel Manor; Eltham Palace; Gray's Inn Gardens; Greenwich Park; Hill Garden; Hyde Park; Osterley Park; Richmond Park; Royal Botanic Gardens; Syon Park; Waterlow Park*

Primulas (Primula spp) : *Golders Hill Park; Richmond Park*

Rhododendrons (Rhododendron spp) : *Cannizaro Park; Chiswick House; Crystal Palace Park; Dulwich Park; Golders Hill Park; Greenwich Park; Hill Garden; Holland Park; Kensington Gardens; Kenwood House; Osterley Park; Richmond Park; Royal Botanic Gardens; Syon Park; Waterlow Park*

Tulips (Tulipa spp) : *Golders Green Crematorium; Hampton Court Palace; Myddelton House; Regent's Park*

Willows (Salix spp) : *Camley Street Natural Park; Holland Park; Hyde Park (The Dell); Museum of London; Ravenscourt Park; Syon Park; Waterlow Park;*

Items of Special Interest

Alpine Beds : *Capel Manor; Golders Green Crematorium; Myddelton House; Royal Botanic Gardens*

Pondside Gardens : *Capel Manor; Golders Hill Park; Hampton Court Palace; Kensington Roof Garden; Mile End Park; Morden Hall Park; Richmond Park; Royal Botanic Gardens; Syon Park; The Watergardens (NGS*)*

Rockery Gardens : *Capel Manor; Chelsea Physic Garden; Eltham Palace; Myddelton House; Rookery Gardens; Royal Botanic Gardens; West Ham Park*

Roof Gardens : *Kensington Roof Garden; Number 1 Poultry; Royal Institute of British Architects*

Spring Bedding : *Cannizaro Park; Chiswick House; Golders Hill Park; Greenwich Park; Hampton Court Palace; Holland Park; Horniman Museum; Hyde Park; Kensington Gardens; Lambeth Palace (NGS*); Lincoln's Inn Fields; Myddelton House; Queen's Park; Regent's Park; Richmond Park; Royal Botanic Gardens; Rookery Gardens; St James's Park; St John's Wood Church; Victoria Park; West Ham Park*

Spring Bulbs : *Brockwell Park; Capel Manor; Carlyle's House; Fenton House; Golders Green Crematorium; Greenwich Park; Horniman Gardens; Lambeth Palace (NGS*); Museum of Garden History; Myddelton House; Roots & Shoots; Royal Botanic Gardens; Trinity Hospice (NGS*)*

Wild Flowers : *Capel Manor; Camley Nature Park; Dulwich Park; East Ham Nature Reserve; Holland Park; Kenwood House; London Wildlife Trust Garden Centre; Mile End Park; Morden Hall Park; Natural History Museum Wildlife Garden; Nunhead Cemetery; Peckham Rye Park; Roots & Shoots; St John's Wood Church; Syon Park; Thames Barrier Park*

Woodland Gardens : *Capel Manor; Chelsea Physic Garden; Holland Park; Kenwood House; Lambeth Palace (NGS*); Morden Hall Park; Nunhead Cemetery; Royal Botanic Gardens; Syon Park*

*Private gardens opening on certain days under the National Gardens Scheme (NGS), see page 30.

**Fields of daffodils planted by the Marie Curie Cancer Care Charity to raise awareness of the needs of cancer patients. Locations of the sites in and around London are listed in the section for Marie Curie Cancer Care 'Fields of Hope' in the main part of the book.

May

Flowers

Azaleas (Azalea spp) : *Cannizaro Park; Dulwich Park; Golders Hill Park; Greenwich Park; Holland Park; Kensington Gardens; 17A Navarino Rd. (NGS*); Richmond Park; Royal Botanic Gardens; Syon Park*

Bluebells (Hyacinthoides non-scripta) : *Kenwood House; Nunhead Cemetery; Osterley Park; Richmond Park; Royal Botanic Gardens; St John's Wood Church; Victoria Park*

Camellias (Camellia spp) : *Chiswick House; Hampton Court Palace; Holland Park; Kensington Gardens; Osterley Park; Richmond Park; Royal Botanic Gardens*

Cherry Blossom (Prunus spp) : *Brockwell Park; Carlyle's House; Crystal Palace Park; Fulham Palace; Golders Hill Park; Gray's Inn Gardens; Kensington Gardens; Hampton Court Palace; Lambeth Community Centre Garden (NGS*); Lincoln's Inn Fields; Middle Temple Gardens; Osterley Park; Ravenscourt Park; Royal Botanic Gardens; St James's Park; St John's Wood Church; Syon Park; Tibetan Peace Garden; Trinity Hospice (NGS*); Victoria Park; West Ham Park; Westminster Abbey Garden;*

Clematis (Clematis spp) [early flowering species] : *Golders Hill Park; Hampton Court Palace; Hill Garden*

Horse Chestnuts (Aesculus spp) : *Golders Hill Park; Great Trees of London; Greenwich Park; Horniman Museum; Hyde Park; Kensal Green Cemetery; Marble Hill Park; Morden Hall Park; Osterley Park; Royal Botanic Gardens*

Irises (Iris spp) : *Holland Park; Myddelton House; Thames Barrier Garden; West Ham Park*

Judas trees (Cercis siliquastrum) : *Fulham Palace; Greenwich Park*

Laburnums (Laburnum spp) : *Cannizaro Park; Golders Hill Park; Hampton Court Palace; Lambeth Community Centre Garden (NGS*); Royal Botanic Gardens*

Lilacs (Syringa spp) : *Carlyle's House; Golders Hill Park; Royal Botanic Gardens, Trinity Hospice (NGS*)*

Magnolias (Magnolia spp) : *Cannizaro Park; Capel Manor; Eltham Palace; Gray's Inn Gardens; Greenwich Park; Hill Garden; Hyde Park; Osterley Park; Richmond Park; Royal Botanic Gardens; Syon Park; Waterlow Park*

Peonies (Paeonia spp) : *Burgh House; Chelsea Physic Garden; Ham House; Myddelton House; Royal Botanic Gardens; West Ham Park*

Rhododendrons (Rhododendron spp) : *Cannizaro Park; Chiswick House; Crystal Palace Park; Dulwich Park; Golders Hill Park; Golders Green Crematorium; Greenwich Park; Hill Garden; Holland Park; Kensington Gardens; Kenwood House; 17A Navarino Rd. (NGS*); Osterley Park; Richmond Park; Royal Botanic Gardens; Syon Park; Waterlow Park*

Tulips (Tulipa spp) : *Golders Green Crematorium; Hampton Court Palace; Myddelton House; Regent's Park*

Wisterias (Wisteria spp) : *Burgh House; Fenton House; Fulham Palace; Hampton Court Palace; Hill Garden; Horniman Museum; Kensington Roof Garden; Lincoln's Inn Fields; Middle Temple Gardens; Myddelton House; 17A Navarino Rd. (NGS*); No.1 Poultry; Rookery Gardens; Trent Country Park*

Items of Special Interest

Alpine Beds : *Capel Manor; Myddelton House; Royal Botanic Gardens*

Herbaceous Borders : *Burgh House; Carlyle's House; Chumleigh Gardens World Garden; Eltham Palace; Emslie Horniman Pleasance Park; Fenton House; Golders Hill Park; Greenwich Park; Hampton Court Palace; Hill Garden; Horniman Museum; Kensington Gardens; Kenwood House; Middle Temple Gardens; Myddelton House; Regent's Park; Rookery Gardens; Royal Botanic Gardens; St James's Park; Syon Park; Thames Barrier Park; Trinity Hospice (NGS*); Waterlow Park;*

Orchards : *Fenton House; Fulham Palace; Rookery Gardens; Waterlow Park*

Pondside Gardens : *Capel Manor; Golders Hill Park; Hampton Court Palace; Kensington Roof Garden; Mile End Park; Morden Hall Park; Richmond Park; Royal Botanic Gardens; Syon Park; The Watergardens (NGS*)*

Wild Flowers : *Capel Manor; Camley Nature Park; Dulwich Park; East Ham Nature Reserve; Holland Park; Kenwood House; London Wildlife Garden Centre; London Wildlife Trust Nature Reserves; Mile End Park; Morden Hall Park; Natural History Museum Wildlife Garden; Nunhead Cemetery; Peckham Rye Park; Roots & Shoots; Royal Botanic Gardens; Syon Park; Thames Barrier Park*

*Private gardens opening on certain days under the National Gardens Scheme (NGS), see page 30.

June

Flowers

Azaleas (Azalea spp) : *Cannizaro Park; Dulwich Park; Golders Hill Park; Greenwich Park; Holland Park; Kensington Gardens; 17A Navarino Rd. (NGS*); Richmond Park; Royal Botanic Gardens; Syon Park*

Clematis (Clematis spp) : *Choumert Square Gardens; Emslie Horniman Pleasance Park; Fenton House; Golders Hill Park; Hampton Court Palace; Hill Garden; Ravencourt Park*

Horse Chestnuts (Aesculus spp) : *Golders Hill Park; Great Trees of London; Greenwich Park; Horniman Museum; Hyde Park; Kensal Green Cemetery; Marble Hill Park; Morden Hall Park; Osterley Park; Royal Botanic Gardens*

Irises (Iris spp) : *Golders Hill Park; Myddelton House; Holland Park; West Ham Park; Thames Barrier Park*

Lavenders (Lavandula spp) : *Carlyle's House; Chelsea Physic Garden; Fenton House; Geffrye Museum; Ham House; Hampton Court Palace; Kensington Roof Gardens; Lambeth Palace* (NGS*); *Mile End Park; Ravenscourt Park; Thames Barrier Park*

Lilacs (Syringa spp) : *Carlyle's House; Golders Hill Park; Rookery Gardens; Royal Botanic Gardens; Royal Hospital Gardens; Trinity Hospice (NGS*)*

Peonies (Paeonia spp) : *Burgh House; Chelsea Physic Garden; Ham House; Myddelton House; Royal Botanic Gardens (Order Beds); West Ham Park*

Poppies (Papaver spp) : *Brockwell Park; Camley Street Nature Park; Tibetan Peace Garden; Thames Barrier Park*

Roses (Rosa spp) : *Cannizaro Park; Capel Manor; Eltham Palace; Fenton House; Golders Green Crematorium; Greenwich Park; Hampton Court Palace; Hill Garden; Holland Park; Horniman Museum; Hyde Park; Kensington Roof Gardens; Lambeth Palace (NGS*); Lincoln's Inn Fields; Middle Temple Gardens; Morden Hall Park; Museum of London Garden; Myddelton House; 17A Navarino Rd. (NGS*); Peckham Rye Park; Ravenscourt Park; Regent's Park; Richmond Park; Rookery Gardens; Roots & Shoots; Royal Botanic Gardens; St James's Park; St John's Wood Church; Syon Park; Tibetan Peace Garden; Victoria Park; West Ham Park*

Waterlilies (Lotus spp) : *Camley Nature Park; Crystal Palace Park; Hill Garden; Kensington Gardens; Myddelton House; Royal Botanic Gardens*

Items of Special Interest

Alpine Beds : *Capel Manor; Myddelton House; Royal Botanic Gardens*

Herbaceous Borders : *Burgh House; Carlyle's House; Choumert Square Gardens; Eltham Palace; Emslie Horniman Pleasance Park; Fenton House; Golders Hill Park; Greenwich Park; Hampton Court Palace; Hill Garden; Horniman Museum; Kensington Gardens; Kenwood House; Middle Temple Gardens; Myddelton House; Postman's Park; Regent's Park; Rookery Gardens; Royal Botanic Gardens; St James Park; St Michael's Convent (NGS*); Syon Park; Trinity Hospice (NGS*); Waterlow Park; Thames Barrier Park*

Old English Gardens : *Battersea Park; Brockwell Park; Ham House; Rookery Gardens; Victoria Park*

Pondside Gardens : *Brockwell Park; Capel Manor; Golders Hill Park; Hampton Court Palace; Kensington Roof Garden; Mile End Park; Morden Hall Park; Richmond Park; Royal Botanic Gardens; Syon Park*

Summer Bedding : *Cannizaro Park; Chiswick House; Golders Hill Park; Greenwich Park; Hampton Court Palace; Holland Park; Horniman Museum; Hyde Park; Kensington Gardens; Lincoln's Inn Fields; Myddelton House; Queen's Park; Regent's Park; Richmond Park; Royal Botanic Gardens; Rookery Gardens; St James's Park; St John's Wood Church; Victoria Park; West Ham Park*

Wild Flowers : *Capel Manor; Camley Nature Park; Dulwich Park; East Ham Nature Reserve; Holland Park; Kenwood House; London Wildlife Garden Centre; London Wildlife Trust Nature Reserves; Mile End Park; Morden Hall Park; Natural History Museum Wildlife Garden: Nunhead Cemetery; Peckham Rye Park; Roots & Shoots; Royal Botanic Gardens; St John's Wood Church; Syon Park; Thames Barrier Park*

*Private gardens opening on certain days under the National Gardens Scheme (NGS), see page 30.

July

Flowers

Clematis (Clematis spp) : *Choumert Square; Emslie Horniman Pleasance Park; Fenton House; Golders Hill Park; Hampton Court Palace; Hill Garden; Ravenscourt Park*

Honeysuckles (Lonicera spp) : *Camley Nature Park; Golders Hill Park; Hampton Court Palace; Hill Garden; Tibetan Peace Garden*

Indian Bean Trees (Catalpa bignonioides) : *Chelsea Physic Garden; Chiswick House; Dulwich Park; Eltham Palace; Horniman Museum; Ravenscourt Park; Trinity Hospice (NGS*)*

Lavenders (Lavandula spp) : *Carlyle's House; Chelsea Physic Garden; Fenton House; Geffrye Museum; Ham House; Hampton Court Palace; Kensington Roof Gardens; Lambeth Palace (NGS*); Mile End Park; Ravenscourt Park; Thames Barrier Park*

Lilies (Lilium spp) : *Golders Hill Park; Lady Venice; Myddelton House*

Roses (Rosa spp) : *Cannizaro Park; Capel Manor; Eltham Palace; Fenton House; Golders Green Crematorium; Greenwich Park; Hampton Court Palace; Hill Garden; Holland Park; Horniman Museum; Hyde Park; Kensington Roof Gardens; Lambeth Palace (NGS*); Lincoln's Inn Fields; Middle Temple Gardens; Morden Hall Park; Museum of London Garden; Myddelton House; 17A Navarino Rd. (NGS*); Peckham Rye Park; Ravenscourt Park; Regent's Park; Richmond Park; Rookery Gardens; Roots & Shoots; Royal Botanic Gardens; Royal Hospital Gardens; St James's Park; St John's Wood Church; Syon Park; Tibetan Peace Garden; Victoria Park; West Ham Park*

Items of Special Interest

Grass Gardens : *Chelsea Physic Garden; Royal Botanic Gardens; Victoria Park*

Herb Gardens : *Battersea Park; Capel Manor; Chelsea Physic Garden; Fenton House; Fulham Palace; Geffrye Museum; Greenwich Park; Kenwood House; Lambeth Palace (NGS*); London Wildlife Trust Garden Centre; Museum of Garden History*

Herbaceous Borders : *Burgh House; Carlyle's House; Choumert Square Gardens; Chumleigh Gardens World Garden; Eltham Palace; Emslie Horniman Pleasance Park; Fenton House; Golders Hill Park; Greenwich Park; Hampton Court Palace; Hill Garden; Horniman Museum; Kensington Gardens; Kenwood House; Middle Temple Gardens; Myddelton House; Regent's Park; Rookery Gardens; Royal Botanic Gardens; St James's Park; Syon Park; Thames Barrier Park; Trinity Hospice (NGS*); Waterlow Park;*

Old English Gardens : *Battersea Park; Brockwell Park; Ham House; Rookery Gardens; Victoria Park*

Pondside Gardens : *Brockwell Park; Capel Manor; Chelsea Physic Garden; Golders Hill Park; Hampton Court Palace; Kensington Roof Garden; Lambeth Palace (NGS*); Mile End Park; Morden Hall Park; Richmond Park; Royal Botanic Gardens; Syon Park*

Scented Gardens : *Chumleigh Gardens World Garden; Chelsea Physic Garden; Fulham Palace; Geffrye Museum; Greenwich Park; Hampton Court Palace; Kensington Roof Gardens; Museum of Garden History; Ravenscourt Park; Royal Botanic Gardens*

Summer Bedding : *Cannizaro Park; Chiswick House; Golders Hill Park; Greenwich Park; Hampton Court Palace; Holland Park; Horniman Museum; Hyde Park; Kensington Gardens; Lincoln's Inn Fields; Myddelton House, Queen's Park; Regent's Park; Richmond Park; Royal Botanic Gardens; Rookery Gardens; St James's Park; St John's Wood Church; Victoria Park; West Ham Park*

Wild Flowers : *Capel Manor; Camley Nature Park; Dulwich Park; East Ham Nature Reserve; Holland Park; Kenwood House; London Wildlife Garden Centre; London Wildlife Trust Nature Reserves; Mile End Park; Morden Hall Park; Natural History Museum Wildlife Garden; Nunhead Cemetery; Peckham Rye Park; Roots & Shoots; Royal Botanic Gardens; St John's Wood Church; Syon Park; Thames Barrier Park*

*Private gardens opening on certain days under the National Gardens Scheme (NGS), see page 30.

August

Flowers

Buddleias (Buddleja spp) : *Camley Nature Park; Crystal Palace Park; St John's Wood Church*

Clematis (Clematis spp) : *Emslie Horniman Pleasance Park; Fenton House; Golders Hill Park; Hampton Court Palace; Hill Garden; Ravenscourt Park*

Dahlias (Dahlia spp) : *Eltham Palace Gardens; Golders Hill Park; Holland Park; Lady Venice*

Fuchsias (Fuchsia spp) : *Hampton Court Palace; Lady Venice*

Pomegranates (Punica granatum) : *Chelsea Physic Garden; Ham House*

Roses (Rosa spp) : *Cannizaro Park; Capel Manor; Eltham Palace; Fenton House; Golders Green Crematorium; Greenwich Park; Hampton Court Palace; Hill Garden; Horniman Museum; Hyde Park; Lambeth Palace (NGS*); Lincoln's Inn Fields; Middle Temple Gardens; Morden Hall Park; Museum of London Garden; Myddelton House; 17A Navarino Rd. (NGS*); No. 1 Poultry; Regent's Park; Richmond Park; Rookery Gardens; Roots & Shoots; Royal Botanic Gardens; Royal Hospital Gardens; St James's Park; St John's Wood Church; Syon Park; Tibetan Peace Garden; Victoria Park; West Ham Park*

Sunflowers (Helianthus spp) : *Emslie Horniman Pleasance Park; Hampton Court Palace; Horniman Museum; Rookery*

Items of Special Interest

Grass Gardens : *Chelsea Physic Garden; Royal Botanic Gardens; Victoria Park*

Great Vine : *Hampton Court Palace*

Herb Gardens : *Battersea Park; Capel Manor; Chelsea Physic Garden; Fulham Palace; Geffrye Museum; Greenwich Park; Kensington Roof Garden; Kenwood House; Lambeth Palace (NGS*); London Wildlife Trust Garden Centre; Museum of Garden History*

Herbaceous Borders : *Chumleigh Gardens World Garden; Eltham Palace; Emslie Horniman Pleasance Park; Fenton House; Golders Hill Park; Greenwich Park; Hampton Court Palace; Horniman Museum; Kensington Gardens; Kensington Roof Gardens; Kenwood House; Middle Temple Gardens; Regent's Park; Rookery Gardens; Royal Botanic Gardens; St James's Park; Syon Park; Trinity Hospice (NGS*); Thames Barrier Park; Waterlow Park*

Pondside Gardens : *Brockwell Park; Capel Manor; Chelsea Physic Garden; Kensington Roof Garden; Morden Hall Park; Richmond Park; Royal Botanic Gardens; Syon House*

Scented Gardens : *Battersea Park; Chelsea Physic Garden; Fulham Palace; Geffrye Museum; Greenwich Park; Hampton Court Palace; Museum of Garden History; Ravenscourt Park; Royal Botanic Gardens*

Summer Bedding : *Cannizaro Park; Chiswick House; Golders Hill Park; Greenwich Park; Hampton Court Palace; Holland Park; Horniman Museum Gardens; Hyde Park; Lincoln's Inn Fields; Queen's Park; Regent's Park; Richmond Park; Royal Botanic Gardens; Rookery Gardens; St James' s Park; St John's Wood Church; Victoria Park; West Ham Park*

*Private gardens opening on certain days under the National Gardens Scheme (NGS), see page 30.

September/October

Flowers

Dahlias (Dahlia spp) : *Eltham Palace Gardens; Golders Hill Park; Holland Park; Lady Venice*

Hydrangeas (Hydrangea spp) : *Eltham Palace; Geffrye Museum; Thames Barrier Park; Tibetan Peace Garden*

Maples (Acer spp) : *Brockwell Park; Cannizaro Park; Crystal Palace Park; Golders Green Crematorium; Golders Hill Park; Greenwich Park; Hampton Court Palace; Hill Garden; Holland Park; Hyde Park; Kenwood House; Osterley Park; Richmond Park; Rookery Gardens; Royal Botanic Gardens; Royal Hospital Gardens; Syon Park; Waterlow Park; West Ham Park*

Michaelmas Daisies (Aster spp) : *Fenton House; Emslie Horniman Pleasance Park; Kensal Green Cemetery; Lady Venice; Rookery Gardens; Tibetan Peace Garden*

Nerine lilies (Nerine spp) : *Hampton Court Palace; Myddelton House*

Items of Special Interest

Autumnal Foliage : *Battersea Park; Brockwell Park; Cannizaro Park; Crystal Palace Park; Fulham Palace; Golders Hill Park; Greenwich Park; Gunnersbury Park; Hampton Court Palace; Hill Garden; Hyde Park; Kensington Gardens; Kenwood House; Myddelton House; Osterley Park; Richmond Park; Regent's Park; Rookery Gardens; Royal Botanic Gardens; Royal Hospital Gardens; St James's Park; Syon Park; Thames Barrier Park; Victoria & Albert Museum Garden; Waterlow Park; West Ham Park*

Great Vine : *Hampton Court Palace*

Japanese Gardens : *Battersea Park; Capel Manor; Holland Park; Royal Botanic Gardens; 17A Navarino Rd. (NGS*)*

Orchards : *Fenton House; Fulham Palace; Rookery Gardens; Waterlow Park*

Peace Gardens : *Tibetan Peace Garden*

Roof Gardens : *Kensington Roof Garden; No. 1 Poultry; Royal Institute of British Architects*

Woodland areas : *Capel Manor; Hill Garden; Holland Park; Kenwood House; Morden Hall Park; Nunhead Cemetery; Royal Botanic Gardens; Syon Park*

*Private gardens opening on certain days under the National Gardens Scheme (NGS), see page 30.

November/December

Flowers

Cedars (Cedrus spp) : *Avenue House Arboretum; Brockwell Park; Chiswick House; Fulham Palace; Greenwich Park; Hampton Court Palace; Osterley Park; Ravenscourt Park; Victoria & Albert Museum Garden*

Coloured Willows (Salix spp) : *Holland Park; Hyde Park (The Dell); Royal Botanic Gardens (Secluded Garden)*

Hollies (Ilex spp) : *Capel Manor; Fenton House; Hampton Court Palace; Kensal Green Cemetery; Kensington Gardens; Royal Botanic Gardens; Osterley Park; Victoria Park; Waterlow Park; West Ham Park*

Winter-flowering cherries (Prunus subhirtella) : *Eltham Palace; Myddelton House; Royal Botanic Gardens*

Witch Hazels (Hamamelis spp) : *Hyde Park (The Dell); Richmond Park (Isabella Plantation); Royal Botanic Gardens (King William's Temple)*

Items of Special Interest

Alpine House : *Capel Manor; Royal Botanic Gardens*

Container Gardens : *Capel Manor; Lady Venice; London Wildlife Garden Centre*

Interesting Evergreens : *Hampton Court Palace; Kensington Gardens; Morden Hall Park; Osterley Park; Royal Hospital Gardens; Royal Botanic Gardens*

Interesting Tree Profiles : *Avenue House Arboretum; Great Trees of London**

Japanese Gardens : *Battersea Park; Capel Manor; Holland Park; Royal Botanic Gardens*

Knot Gardens, Parterres & Topiary :

Knot Gardens *Capel Manor; Fulham Palace; Hampton Court Palace; Museum of Garden History*

Parterres *Ham House; Hampton Court Palace; Royal Botanic Gardens*

Topiary *Capel Manor; Ham House; Hampton Court Palace; Museum of Garden History; Syon Park; Thames Barrier Park*

Mazes : *Capel Manor; Crystal Palace Park; Hampton Court Palace*

Peace Gardens : *Tibetan Peace Garden*

Roof Gardens : *Kensington Roof Garden; No. 1 Poultry; Royal Institute of British Architects*

Tropical Conservatories : *Avery Hill; Barbican; Capel Manor; Royal Botanic Gardens; Myddelton House; Syon Park*

*Great Trees in London registered as 'special' due to either their great age, size, extraordinary shape, cultural or historical significance or particular importance to wildlife.

The location for 6 of these is listed in the section for 'Great Trees of London' in the main part of the book.

Certain privately-owned gardens generously
open to the public on specific days each year to raise
money for charity.   The project is run by the National Gardens Scheme
(NGS) and involves approximately 3,500 gardens throughout England
and Wales. The gardens opening under the Scheme, their details and
dates of opening are published each year by the NGS in a book entitled,
"Gardens of England and Wales Open for Charity", which is available in
all large bookshops.   You can also obtain a leaflet for the near 200
London gardens opening under the Scheme by sending a stamped
addressed A5 envelope and 50p worth of stamps to the
NGS County Organiser:
Mrs Maurice Snell, Moleshill House,
The Fairmile, Cobham, Surrey, KT11 1BG.

With so many places to visit and
opening dates spread from March to October it is
difficult to pick out a small representative handful to describe
here. Those chosen give some idea of the range of NGS gardens
to be found in the London area. I have included most of the ones
that belong to institutions as these are less likely to move than the
many private gardens that feature in the scheme.

A-Z list of Gardens

With description & visitor information

AVENUE HOUSE ARBORETUM

Address: East End Road, Finchley, London N3; Tel: 020 8359 2019; **Owner:** London Borough of Barnet; **Transport**: Finchley Central tube (Northern Line); Bus 13,82,143,143A,260; **Entrance**: Free; **Opening Times**: Daily, 8am-dusk; **Other Information**: Car parking off East End Road, dogs welcome, museum, toilets, tree trail; **Seasonal Features**: January, February, November, December; cedars; interesting tree profiles

This is in the grounds of a Victorian mansion built in 1859 and endowed with a fine tree collection by Henry Charles Stephens, son of Dr Henry Stephens who invented ink. The mansion, Avenue House, still stands rather imposingly at the entrance but the grounds have sadly lost their former glory. A number of rare and unusual trees do however remain and these can be sought out with the help of a printed tree trail available from the museum in the old house (open Tues, Wed, Thurs 2-4.30pm).

In front of the mansion a sloping lawn leads down to a small overgrown pond. In the shrubbery adjacent to East End Road a venerable weeping beech steadily and silently spreads it's pendulous limbs. Three of the tree's early branches have now bent right down to the ground and then rooted, sending up new trees to continue the line. For spring blossom, the Judas and southern nettle tree are the most effusive while, for autumn colour, the Hungarian oak and Italian maple stand out. In winter a variety of conifers and some intriguing, contorted tree skeletons dominate the landscape.

The park is generally tranquil despite being surrounded by busy roads. On Tues, Wed and Thurs afternoons there is the added attraction of a museum in Avenue House manned by friendly volunteers. This tells the story of members of the Stephens family who lived in the house, created the park and then donated both to the people of Finchley in 1918.

AVERY HILL PARK WINTER GARDENS

Address: University of Greenwich, Bexley Road, Eltham, London SE9; **Tel**: 020 8331 8000; **Owner**: University of Greenwich; **Location**: Avery Hill Park; **Transport**: Falconwood, New Eltham train stations; Bus 132,233; **Entrance**: Free; **Opening Times**: Mon-Thurs 1-4pm, Fri 1-3pm, Sat & Sun 10am-4pm. Closed 24, 25 Dec, 1 Jan; **Other Information**: Aviary, cafe, disabled access, dogs welcome in restricted areas, parking, toilets; **Seasonal Features**: January, February, November, December; bougainvillea, tropical conservatories

1. A bright splash of spring blossom in St James' Park frames Buckingham Palace
2. A sweeping view across south London from the colourful Horniman Museum Gardens

3. Stately cedars of Lebanon characterise Osterley Park

5. *opposite:* The striking and the exotic thrive in Kensington Flower Walk in Hyde Park

4. A blanket of May colour in the Isabella Plantation in Richmond Park

6. *main picture;* The last rays of an autumn sun fall on the Palm House pond in the Royal Botanic Gardens, Kew

7. *left:* The Ionic temple of Chiswick House Gardens perfectly reflected in the lake.

8. *opposite:* The great conservatory of Syon Park towers majestically above surrounding lawns

10. A fleeting summer's moment by a hidden pond in the Watergardens

11. *opposite:* The centrepiece fountain and statue of Hercules and Achelous in the Palm House pond at the Royal Botanic Gardens, Kew

9. *main picture:* A watery spectrum of green foliage in Syon Park

12. Colourful bedding in the formal garden in Holland Park

13. The grand pergola of the intriguingly beautiful Hill Garden of Hampstead

In the late 19th century a sumptuous Italianate style villa was built on Avery Hill by Colonel John North, a magnate dealing in Chilean nitrates. This individual had wealth and flaunted it. As an integral part of his mansion, he commissioned a splendid Winter Garden consisting of three giant conservatories. These were designed by T. W. Cutler in 1891 and stand today as the best London survival of this extravagant Victorian type of building. The house itself was badly damaged in the blitz and what remains is in the hands of the University of Greenwich, as indeed are the Winter Gardens which have been badly under-funded and the contents poorly maintained in recent years. However the structures themselves are grand, in particular the central, domed temperate house which holds a rampant, 27 metre high bougainvillea and a massive, 18 metre high date palm.

To either side of the cathedralesque temperate house are smaller conservatories – one cool and one tropical. Towering, flaccid banana plants, staghorn ferns, bromeliads, coffee and citrus plants are found in the hotter of the two while a central goldfish pond with bamboos, spring-flowering camellias and more familiar semi-tropical species fill the other. Returning to the main temperate house, the sense of decaying grandeur is somewhat unavoidable but there are some botanical giants of a remarkable age that complement the wonderful structure designed for them. Giant euphorbias totter nervously and a huge banyan tree, many palms and other weird cacti, aroids and succulents of various forms all prickle and jostle for position. A little display of old gardening memorabilia is gathered on one side, but underfunding has meant labelling is scarce. This is a place with much potential; the structure is there as are as many of the plants, though some have suffered through lack of resources.

BARBICAN CONSERVATORY

Address: The Barbican, Silk Street, London EC2; **Tel**: 020 7638 4141; **Owner**: City of London; **Location**: Barbican Centre 3rd Floor; **Transport**: Barbican tube (Metropolitan, Hamm. & City, Circle Lines); Bus 8,11,15, 23,25; **Entrance**: Free; **Opening Times**: Sundays & Bank Hols 10am-5.30pm; **Other Information**: Art gallery, Barbican Centre entertainment facilities, cafes, disabled access, no dogs, toilets; **Seasonal Features**: January, February, November, December; semi-tropical conservatory, cacti collection

Once in the Barbican Centre you have only to take the lift to the third floor and you will quickly find yourself in a leafy, semi-tropical world where primitive tree ferns abound and a massive date palm has grown almost 12 metres tall. The Barbican's conservatory was opened in 1984 and rises up through four floors of the Barbican Centre to a glass roof at the top. It has three balconies on one side from which weeping figs hang like curtains over the side. On the second level an arid house contains an impressive cacti collection which includes a giant cactus (*Carnegiea gigantea*), the largest of all the cacti species.

A long flowering bougainvillea climbs high up the conservatory wall and produces brightly coloured blossom, as do the passionflowers and hibiscus plants. Coconut palms, kentia palms, rubber trees, bananas and bamboos all flourish in this lush, tropical paradise; and lower down, you will find many familiar cheeseplants, bromeliads and spathiphyllums. A huge banyan tree dominates the eastern section and an aviary and ponds with Koi carp and terrapins help entertain the children. With a mixture of the exotic, the huge and familiar, and one of the City's best cacti collections, this is an impressive indoor garden with interesting features all year round.

BATTERSEA PARK

Address: Battersea, London SW I I; **Tel**: 020 8871 7530; **Owner**: Wandsworth Borough Council; **Location**: South bank of Thames, west of Chelsea Bridge; **Transport**: Sloane Square tube (District & Circle Lines); Battersea Park train station; Bus 44,137,137A,344; **Entrance**: Free; **Opening Times**: Daily, 7am-dusk; **Other Information**: Cafe, disabled access, dogs welcome, parking, shop, toilets; **Seasonal Features**: June, July, August, September, October; festival gardens, old english garden, herb garden, autumnal trees.

Battersea Park is now one of London's main parks; though it has had a relatively short and chequered history. It was laid out by the Victorians on poor quality land in central London that was wet, marshy and unfit for anything other than occasional market garden plots and Sunday trade fairs. In previous centuries Battersea Fields was a place of crime and violence but in the mid 1800's the Victorian authorities decided to try and clean up the area and they drained the land, dug out a lake and planted trees.

Battersea Park was opened to the public in 1858 and by 1900 had become fashionable with horse-drawn carriages filling the broad drives. It was used as a main centre for the Festival of Britain in 1951 when the festival gardens with their astounding fountains were installed. In 1985 the magnificent Peace Pagoda was erected overlooking both the river and the park. This is 12 metres in height and is a gift to the people of London from the Japanese Order Nipponzan Mayohoji.

Within the 80 hectares that form the park today one can find a riverside walk with Japanese pagoda, a boating lake with Victorian pump house and cascades, a Victorian bandstand and a series of eye-catching sculptures. There is a huge old strawberry tree, one of the Capital's Great Trees, residing by the lake and the tallest weeping ash in the country not far away. Individual gardens where one can relax include the festival gardens with their wonderful fountains, and the nearby tranquil old english garden sheltered by a wall and large trees. In summer this is a profusion of aroma and colour filled with lavender, roses, lilies, and irises. There is also a nature reserve, a banked wilderness area screening traffic and a subtropical garden created in 1863 with palms, tree ferns and bananas in raised beds. Tucked away by one of the main carriage drives is the horticultural therapy garden known as 'THRIVE' which was built by the Disabled Living Foundation which now runs courses on the cultivation and use of plants. (Tel. 020 7720 2212)

Battersea Park also caters for many sporting activities. There are tennis courts, an athletics track, a bowling green, sports pitches and a simple 'trim trail' which anyone can use. Children can be let loose in one of several playgrounds or taken to the zoo and there is always the cafe situated by the lake where one can recuperate. All in all, Battersea Park is fun to visit with many varied attractions. It provides plant lovers with some unusual trees, there is a printed 'tree trail' guide available in the pump house, and the local community with a much needed interesting green space.

BROCKWELL PARK

Address: Tulse Hill, London SE24; **Tel**: 020 7926 0105; **Owner**: London Borough of Lambeth; **Transport**: Brixton tube (Victoria Line); Herne Hill train station; Bus 2,3,37,68,68A,196,322; **Entrance**: Free; **Opening Times**: Daily, 9am-dusk; **Other Information**: Cafe, disabled access, dogs welcome outside walled garden, toilets; **Seasonal Features**: June, July, September, October; old english garden, autumnal trees

Brockwell Park was opened in 1892 and is today the largest green space in Lambeth, with a pretty and secluded old english walled garden, three ponds and far reaching views towards the City and East End. It is a popular park and provides the local community with sports facilities, an outdoor gym, a lido and a community greenhouse at which childcare is provided if booked in advance.

The large walled garden is a kaleidoscope of colours with almost year-round interest, though it does suffer from lack of maintenance. When it was first planted up, in the 1890's, all the plants used were those that had been mentioned in Shakespeare's plays. Yew hedges, holly, eucalyptus, box and broom provide permanent structure and cover for wildlife. A large, gnarled black mulberry tree leans menacingly over one of the paths and nearby is a *Clerodendrum trichotomum* which produces startling orange and turquoise-blue fruits in autumn. With its pergolas, yew hedges and red brick walls cloaked in climbing shrubs, the walled garden is a lush and peaceful haven.

Brockwell Park covers a gently sloping hill which is worth climbing on a clear day for the panoramic city views to be had from the top. There is also a cafe, an open air theatre, an attractive clock tower, some summer bedding and several good specimen cedars and oaks on the hilltop. On the eastern edge of the park, beyond the walled garden and aviary, are a line of three ponds. Thirty species of bird have been observed on the larger duck pond and beside the shady path around the other two lakes you will find a large Caucasian wingnut and sweet gum, both of which have beautiful autumnal foliage. In spring the lesser periwinkle forms a carpet of purple by the lower pond and during the summer yellow flag irises and pendulous sedge flower by the waterside.

With its undulating grassland, stands of ancient trees and large, walled garden tinged with decaying grandeur, Brockwell Park provides large open spaces, fine views of the City and peaceful, secluded areas. It is a valuable resource for locals and wildlife alike.

BURGH HOUSE GARDEN

Address: Burgh House, New End Square, Hampstead, London NW3; **Tel**: 020 7431 0144; **Owner**: Camden Borough Council; **Transport**: Hampstead tube (Northern Line); Hampstead Heath train station; Bus 46,268; **Entrance**: Free; **Opening Times**: Wed-Sun, 12pm-5pm, Closed Mon & Tues; (tel to check opening times) **Other Information**: Cafe (open Wed-Sun, 11am-5.30pm), disabled access to garden, no dogs, toilets; **Seasonal Features**: May, June; herbaceous borders, wisteria

Burgh House is one of the oldest houses in Hampstead, built in 1703 or 1704. Dr. George Williamson, an international art expert, lived here from 1906-1924 and commissioned Gertrude Jekyll to design the garden. During the Second World War Burgh House was mostly empty and lucky to escape bomb damage. In 1979, restored by the Council and refurbished by the Burgh House Trust, it opened to the public as the attractive house, garden and museum that you see today.

The house itself is a Queen Anne Grade I Listed Building much used by the local community as a venue for concerts, art exhibitions, meetings and parties. Visitors are welcome to amble round its music room, library and art gallery and are able to see many of the original 18th century features. You may also climb the old staircase to the Hampstead Museum on the first floor or descend to the basement buttery for mouth-watering home-cooking that can be eaten in the garden on a fine day.

Of the original Jekyll garden unfortunately only the terrace around the front and side of the house remains. The wrought iron entrance gates were added in the 1720s by Dr. William Gibbons, who lived in Burgh House at the time. He was the physician to the famous spa at Hampstead Wells to which people flocked to drink the foul-tasting but allegedly medicinal waters. Enter these gates and you are welcomed by a profusion of floral colour and texture, together with the pleasant prospect of Well Walk as it is today.

An ancient wisteria has entwined itself around railings leading up to the front door and forms an oasis of colour each May along with the surrounding clematis. The garden's herbaceous borders are planted for year round colour with daffodils, primulas and hyacinths all giving a vivid spring display, a massive peony and irises blooming in May, and abundant roses, alyssum, delphiniums, asters, phlox and foxgloves stealing the show in mid summer. A millstone path with diamond patterns leads round the front of the house to the shadier side garden where a bay tree, flowering cherry, cypress and bamboo give shelter and an elegant, little fountain below the front door lends added interest.

Since 1979, volunteers have transformed Burgh House terrace from a neglected, derelict weedbed to an attractive garden of fresh colour. In five months the land was cleared and over 100 varieties of flowers planted, which have flourished to produce beds amongst which it is a pleasure to sit and escape the cares of modern life.

CAMLEY STREET NATURE PARK

Address: 12 Camley Street, London NW1; **Tel**: 020 7833 2311; **Owner**: London Wildlife Trust; **Transport**: Kings Cross tube (Metropolitan, Hamm. & City, Circle, Piccadilly, Victoria, Northern Lines) & train station; Bus 46,214,C12; **Entrance**: Free; **Opening Times**: Mon – Thurs 9.00am – 5.00 pm, Sat & Sun 10.00am – 4.00pm (winter), 11.00am –5.00pm (summer), Closed on Fri; **Other Information**: Visitor centre/classroom, toilets, no dogs; **Seasonal Features**: April, May, June; summer meadow, wild flowers, marsh marigolds, waterlilies, pondside garden

Cannizaro Park

In some ways the most rewarding of plant havens to visit are those in urban areas where they are least expected. The Camley Street Nature Reserve certainly qualifies as one of these; it is a thriving wildlife haven well hidden among the heavy industry and pollution of London's Kings Cross. Screened from the adjacent scrapyards and busy railway lines by thriving thickets of willows, alders, aspen and rowans, and with its pond continually topped up by the canal which snakes along its eastern boundary, it is a fertile spot supporting a large amount of plant and bird life.

A wild flower meadow which is on your right as you enter the park is beautiful from April to late May when it is cut to encourage species diversity. Primroses, cowslips and bluebells flower there in March and April and the common spotted orchid and lesser broomrape have both found their own way to the reserve, but do not appear every year. Another springtime favourite is the dazzling marsh marigold. A path snakes down through the reserve with the canal lying quietly on one side and leads you into a green oasis of flourishing herbs, poppies, reeds, buddleias, honeysuckle and rambling roses.

Depending on the time of year there is an abundance of blossom or fruit to see, birds such as wagtails, tits, robins and wrens are at home here and even black redstarts and kingfishers have been recorded. At the bottom of the reserve a large pond is a lovely place to sit and watch the coots and moorhens dabbling in the clear water, remarkably undisturbed by the adjacent scrap metal yard. In June and July the white waterlilies are in full bloom in the pond and the yellow flag iris and club-rushes by the pond are at their best. From then to September when the leaves begin to turn there is much buddleia and many different woodland and climbing plants flowering in the reserve along with colourful fruits.

The office and workroom are well run and whenever you visit you will find the staff friendly and helpful. A visit to Camley Street Natural Park is interesting and worthwhile and it is inspiring to see just how many species can survive remarkably stress-free amongst the pollution and noise of a modern day industrial city.

CANNIZARO PARK

Address: West Side Common,Wimbledon, London SW19; **Tel**: 020 8946 7349; **Owner**: London Borough of Merton; **Transport**:Wimbledon tube (District Line) & train station; Bus 93,200; **Entrance**: Free; **Opening Times**: Daily, Mon-Fri 8am-dusk, Sat, Sun & Bank Hols 9am-dusk; **Other Information**: Dogs welcome, events, toilets; **Seasonal**

Features: January, February, March, April, May, June, July, September, October; snowdrops, heather, crocuses, daffodils, rhododendrons, azaleas, roses, formal bedding, maples

This is a real treasure lying on the edge of Wimbledon Common with a grand gated entrance leading to a driveway flanked by neat and colourful flower beds. This will take you up to Cannizaro House and its former grounds, now owned by the Council and converted to a beautifully maintained public park. The park is horticulturally very interesting with a well established and varied collection of trees and an attractive range of flowering plants.

There are some cork oaks, sassafras and mulberry trees, all remarkable for their age, and in autumn the foliage is ablaze with some fine red Japanese maples. Time can be spent lazing on the lawns between the trees or wandering the woods in the southern end of the park – a sea of colour in late spring. You may also like to visit the pool and stroll round the formal or wild gardens around Cannizaro House in which there is a cafe.

For a relatively small park there is a long flowering season. A heather garden and snowdrop glade bloom at the start of the year, crocus beds in March and a daffodil walk in April. The azalea dell and rhododendrons are spectacular in May and June when the walled rose garden is also most attractive. To conclude, Cannizaro is well maintained with lovely old trees and beautiful magnolias, azaleas and rhododendrons. It very pleasant to relax and spend time here.

CAPEL MANOR GARDENS

Address: Bullsmoor Lane, Enfield EN1; **Tel**: 020 8366 4442; **Owner**: Capel Manor College; **Location**: By Jnct. 25 of M25; **Transport**: Turkey Street train station; **Entrance**: Entrance charge, tel. for details; **Opening Times**: Mar-Oct, daily, 10.00am-6.00pm; Nov-Feb, weekdays (tel. for times & special events); **Other Information**: Animal world, cafe, disabled access, dogs on leads only, gardening classes, guided walks, parking, plants for sale at special events, shop; **Seasonal Features**: January, February, March, April, May, June, July, August, September, October, November, December; topiary, winter beds, alpines, hollies, maze, achilleas, magnolias, roses, colour gardens, designer gardens, Gardening Which? demonstration gardens, historic gardens, Japanese garden, rock garden, spring garden, wild flowers

Thirty acres of colour, exuberance and horticultural creativity are what lies beside the busy A10 in the grounds of the attractive Georgian Capel Manor. The house is now the headquarters of London's only agricultural college and its red brick stable block is central to an animal world where you can see rare breeds which are used for husbandry and training purposes. The gardens have continual seasonal interest from the topiary garden, Japanese garden, maze, winter colour beds, tropical display house and holly collection in mid winter to a multitude of summer highlights. Areas of year round interest include the National Gardening Centre with a myriad of show gardens, and at least 34 regularly updated demonstration and themed gardens sponsored by the 'Gardening Which?' magazine. Both these sections are packed with the latest plant cultivars and design ideas for gardeners to view in situ.

A tour round Capel Manor National Gardening Centre will take you past a large and busy display of walling, bedding, paving, garden furniture, etc., some in better condition than others, but most in show gardens with well known sponsors. The Japanese garden here is interesting, a low allergen garden shows how to lessen risks of hay fever by discarding wind pollinated plants and a Cornish garden with an Impressionistic planting plan was designed to celebrate the total eclipse of the sun in 1999.

In the 'Gardening Which?' area demonstration gardens trials are run on pesticides and fertilisers and many colour schemes are explored. The National Collection of *Achillea spp* (yarrow or bachelor's buttons) is held here and there is an A-Z shrub collection and eight themed gardens including a family garden and container, water and wildlife gardens.

Up near the old Capel Manor stable block you will find a large pond surrounded by crocosmia, bog iris, corkscrew willow and reed mace and stocked with golden orfe. It is a slightly noisy but attractive place to relax and view the lake, stables, animal farm and colourful spring and summer display of bedding plants before you.

At the top of the lake is a rose garden planted in 1996 which is worth a visit in mid summer and down one side of the lake runs a pleached lime avenue. To complete a tour of Capel Manor there are several less crowded areas; the themed gardens, historic gardens, wilderness and the woodland walk. The themed gardens include a topiary garden, a pine walk, a sensory garden, and gardens for the disabled. The historic gardens cover a large, informal area immediately around Capel Manor House and display a variety of styles, starting with the early 15th century herb garden. Some are ageless, e.g. the spring wild garden, but others such as the ha-ha and knot garden belong to a specific era. An Italian holly maze and tropical house give winter interest and this area is spacious and relaxing, in contrast to the formality of the show gardens. If you still have the energy there is a wooded wilderness area hiding a folly and summer glade and a woodland walk with stately specimen trees planted by the Victorians. This last includes a notable holly collection, a temple folly and a carpet of spring bulbs.

Capel Manor is full of the latest gardening tips and plants on the market and even those currently on trial. It is educational and inspiring, providing horticultural interest throughout the year, but does take time and effort to complete in one visit. Season tickets for Friends of Capel are available on request as are details of many courses and special events. You can obviously pick and choose what to see, depending on your interest and the time of year, but it is worth your while trying to reach the historic gardens towards the end of the tour, where you can unwind and leave the present behind for a while.

CARLYLE'S HOUSE GARDEN

Address: 24 Cheyne Row, London SW3; **Tel**: 020 7352 7087; **Owner**: The National Trust; **Transport**: Sloane Square tube station (District & Circle Lines); Bus 11,19,22, 49,239; **Entrance**: Entrance charge; **Opening Times**: 27 Mar-31 Oct, Wed-Fri 2pm-5pm, Sat, Sun & Bank Hols 11am – 5pm (last admission 4.30pm); **Other Information**: No dogs; **Seasonal Features**: May, June, July; Victorian town garden with on-going restoration, lilacs, vines, herbaceous borders

Seek out Thomas Carlyle's modest town house at 24 Cheyne Row in Chelsea and you will be able to step back in time and explore the home, garden and personal lives of Carlyle (1795-1881) and his wife, Jane (1801-1866), from 1834 until their deaths. The National Trust has preserved the rooms, furniture and many personal relics in good condition and these include a lush and colourful little Victorian town garden where Thomas Carlyle spent much time meditating and smoking his pipe.

In the end wall to Carlyle's Garden some of the original Tudor brickwork can still be seen. Elsewhere the high walls are covered over with vines and Virginia creeper and overhung with a large acacia. A Victorian planting theme reflecting that present during Carlyle's lifetime is ongoing and the garden still contains a walnut tree, cherry, vines and lilac bushes all of which Carlyle recorded in various letters he wrote to relatives in Scotland. A small, central, rectangular lawn is surrounded by a gravel path and around the walls runs a lush, herbaceous border which is itself bordered by short box hedging. The corner nearest the house is shaded by a large fig tree and a pear tree blossoms in spring along with many spring bulbs. The border contains a mixture of ferns, hostas, lavender, irises, lungwort, marigolds, hydrangea, honesty and globe thistles. Though small, it is interesting to step back in time and see a garden unchanged in its design for over a century but still in such good condition.

CHELSEA PHYSIC GARDEN

Address: 66 Royal Hospital Road, Chelsea, London SW3; **Tel**: 020 7352 5646; **Owner**: Chelsea Physic Garden Company; **Transport**: Sloane Square tube (District & Circle Lines); Bus 239 (not suns); **Entrance**: Entrance charge; **Opening Times**: April-Oct, Wed 12-5pm, Sun 2-6pm; during Chelsea Flower Show 12-5pm; some winter Sundays (tel. for details); **Other Information**: Disabled access, no dogs, events, plant sales, shop, teas, toilets; **Seasonal Features**: February, June, July, August; snowdrop weekends, herb and medicinal gardens, peonies, rockery

This secret three and a half acre garden tucked away behind its red brick wall in Swan Walk, Chelsea, was founded in 1673 when London's Society of Apothecaries established it to grow and study the plants of their trade. The garden was bought as part of the Manor of Chelsea and restored by Sir Hans Sloane in 1722. It was then leased back to the Apothecaries at an annual rent of £5, a figure that remains the same today although an independent charity is now in charge. Philip Miller, gardener from 1722 to 1770, made Chelsea the world's finest botanic garden of its time with plants from all around the globe.

Venture inside the garden's boundary wall and you will be rewarded by an oasis of history and a beautifully kept profusion of rare and interesting plants. Some of the trees are the original 17th Century specimens and include a contorted black mulberry tree, the largest olive in Britain, a bay and a Mediterranean pomegranate. A large golden rain tree towers over the regimental flowerbeds and droops with yellow blossom in July.

There are various glasshouses including the newly restored cool fernery which commemorates the curator, Thomas Moore, who helped to start the Victorian craze for ferns. A large collection of sage (*Salvia spp*) has been built up and many *Cistus spp* flower abundantly in June. One set of flowerbeds are laid out so as to contain only plants from the same biological families and others have solely herbs, dye plants, poisonous plants, Mediterranean curiosities, aromatics or native British plants. Signs are both discrete and clear and complement the neat borders. In the centre of the garden the paternal statue of the benefactor Sir Hans Sloane keeps a watchful eye from its pedestal.

A history of medicine garden contains plants that have yielded major pharmaceutical drugs in the past and those that continue to be used in medical research today. One of the most interesting little flower displays at Chelsea contains flowers used in the ancient theory of the 'Doctrine of Signatures' which stipulated that certain plants were 'signed' by a beneficent God so as to indicate which disorders they would cure. As an example, perforate St John's wort, which is grown in this bed, has perforated leaves and was used to treat dagger wounds. A peaceful stroll around Chelsea enables you to rediscover some lost history and acts as a gentle reminder of the importance of plants in our lives, which we all tend to take for granted.

CHISWICK HOUSE GARDEN   *See illustration 7, between pages 32 and 33*

Address: Chiswick House, Burlington Lane, Chiswick, London, W4; **Tel:** 020 8995 5390; **Owner**: London Borough of Hounslow and English Heritage; **Transport**: Chiswick train station; Turnham Green & Chiswick Park tubes (District Line); Bus 190,425,E3; **Entrance**: Free; **Opening Times**: Gardens open daily 8.30am-dusk: House open April-Oct, daily 10am-6pm (dusk if earlier); Nov-Mar, daily 10am-4pm. Closed 24-26 Dec; **Other Information**: Cafe, dogs welcome everywhere but the Italian garden, parking, theatre in the amphitheatre, tree trail leaflets from Grounds information centre; **Seasonal Features**: March, April, June, July, August; camellias, formal bedding

Chiswick House, itself a masterpiece of 18th century Palladian architecture, stands boldly amidst classical grounds full of expansive lawns, remarkable vistas, avenues and follies. Richard Boyle, 3rd Earl of Burlington, built the house in 1727–29 and William Kent designed the gardens with humour and artistic flair. Within a comparatively small area you will find a snaking canal with rustic bridge and recently restored cascade, avenues of grandiose spreading cedars, stone urns and sphinxes, an Italian garden with conservatory and formal flower beds, a Doric column, a wilderness area and much else. A domed temple overlooks a garden which drops down in circular terraces to a pool with an obelisk where Kent is said to have spent the whole night in meditation. In the conservatory there are over 40 camellia bushes, some of which date back to the early 19th century – a national treasure in the eyes of many.

The camellias blossom from March to May and the bedding that fronts their Italian conservatory is a picture from March through till August. In spring the rhododendrons and woodland areas surrounding the lawns burst into colour as undergrowth and trees flower before the leaf canopy fully unfurls to shut off much of the sunlight. This leaf canopy can often be appreciated in autumn when some older trees such as ginkgo, oak, sweet gum and the catalpa by the house turn spectacular autumnal colours before shedding their leaves in October. Large cedars and other evergreens retain their foliage to give structure and interest throughout winter.

CHOUMERT SQUARE GARDENS

Address: Choumert Square, London SE15; **Owner**: The Residents; **Location**: Via wrought iron gates off Choumert Grove; **Transport**: Peckham Rye train station; Bus 12,36,37,63,78,171,312,345; **Entrance**: Free apart from NGS open day; Opening Times: All year (for official NGS open day see NGS book); **Other Information**: Disabled access, guide dogs only, on NGS* open day there are plant sales, refreshments and stalls; **Seasonal Features**: June, July; herbaceous borders

This consists of a paved walkway up a row of 46 old brewery worker's houses all with their small adjacent front gardens burgeoning with plants. You enter from Choumert Grove through wrought iron gates with an attendant eucalyptus tree and are immediately in a very different, soft and leafy environment. As you make your way down the path, between the gardens, plants reach out from all sides. Climbing roses overhang your route, potted herbs and shrubs loom behind you, bright window boxes catch the corner of your eye and a powerful blaze of flowers lights your way ahead. At the far end is a rectangular communal garden with plenty of seating and picnic tables where residents hold summer parties. A pretty acacia offers some welcome shade here, as does a larger acacia halfway down the row whose gnarled trunk has to be negotiated by the nearest resident before they can enter their hobbit-like house behind.

Once rested amongst the flowerbeds and wisteria and jasmine covered walls in the small communal garden, you need to take the same sensuous floral walk to exit. Borders between the gardens blur into a colourful, leafy haze as scramblers, shrubs and overflowing pots obscure the fences and paving slabs. On the National Garden Scheme open day many residents sit in their gardens serving homemade refreshments and some have open house art galleries. The gate is open for garden visitors throughout the year though the gardens look at their most colourful in mid summer and it is on the official NGS open day that you will experience the full urban village atmosphere of Choumert Square.

*National Garden Scheme – for details see page 30

CHUMLEIGH MULTICULTURAL GARDEN

Address: Chumleigh Gardens Almshouses, Chumleigh Street, Burgess Park, London SE5; **Tel:** 020 7525 1050; **Transport**: Elephant & Castle tube (Northern & Bakerloo Lines); Bus 12,35,40,45,45A,68,171,176,184,343; **Entrance**: Free; **Opening Times**: Mon-Fri 10am-5pm, Sat & Sun 10am-5pm (dusk if earlier); **Other Information**: Cafe, no dogs, events, guided tours, parking; **Seasonal Features**: April, May, July, August; English, Oriental, African & Caribbean, Islamic and Mediterranean gardens

The attractive almshouses at Chumleigh were built in 1821 by the Friendly Female Society. They are now managed by the Parks Ranger Service on behalf of the London Borough of Southwark, and provide a visitor centre with a cafe and conference centre for hire. Their walled gardens incorporate five individual garden styles from around the world which show how plants are adapted to different environments and how they are used in various cultures. The five styles on view are English, Oriental, African and Caribbean, Islamic and Mediterranean.

The English garden is traditional and contains the ever popular lawn edged with mixed herbaceous beds planted to give a long flowering season. Generously planted tubs line the paths and the almshouses overlooking the lawn are adorned with hanging baskets and a crimson glory vine. The vine turns a deep crimson in autumn and one can admire this garden through mid and late summer.

The peaceful Oriental garden is designed to represent a miniature landscape with mountains, woods and water. Many of the plants are grown for their interesting foliage. In the African and Caribbean garden the hardier species such as tree ferns, bamboos and Japanese banana set the scene. Arum lilies and red-hot pokers all add interest as does a desert area which includes cacti and succulents.

The Islamic garden is dominated by a blue mosaic pool with a large jelly palm at its centre. A trachycarpus palm stands, sentry-like, in each corner and an arbour draped in grape vine leads into the Mediterranean section. This is a fragrant garden with many familiar herbs and an arbour supporting climbing grapes, roses and an exotic, orange-flowered trumpet creeper. A large yucca, broom, alliums and other drought tolerant species flourish in the flower beds.

These gardens provide a brief insight into various gardens around the world. They are also secluded and peaceful, looking at their best in spring and summer.

COLUMBIA ROAD FLOWER MARKET

Address: Columbia Road, London E2; **Transport**: Shoreditch tube (East London Line), Bus 5,8,26,35,43,37,38,55,67,78,149,242,243A; **Entrance**: Free; **Opening Times**: Sunday 9am-2pm; **Other Information**: Cafes, disabled access, dogs welcome, shops, toilets; **Seasonal Features**: Cut flowers, garden plants, house plants

Every Sunday Columbia Road in London's East End comes alive in a blaze of colour and feverish activity as people haggle and jostle for some of the cheapest plants and flowers in the Capital. You'll find everything from seeds to tree ferns, bedding plants to garden tools, cut flowers to trees and if you really want a bargain – buy in bulk. If you're trying not to buy it is a vibrant horticultural riot in which to set eyes on the entire range of what is green and can be physically bought and sold in a crowded city street.

As you wend your way through the market you will pass massive palms, alpines, large grasses, orchids, standard trees, ferns, remarkable topiary shapes, bamboos, cacti, climbers, bromeliads, etc., etc. Endless buckets of colourful fresh and dried cut flowers brighten the pavements and flower arranging materials, containers and contorted twigs are not forgotten. Vegetables, herbs, bedding plants, compost and all sorts of gardening paraphernalia can be found at many stalls and in some small shops in adjacent streets.

The market blossoms in the morning, reaches a climax at about noon and winds down about 2 pm when the best bargains can be struck with increasingly ratty stall holders. Afterwards you can unwind by relaxing with a pint and a bite to eat in one of the nearby, authentic East End pubs.

CRYSTAL PALACE PARK

Address: Crystal Palace Road, London SE22; **Tel**: 020 8778 7148; **Owner**: Bromley Council; **Transport**: Crystal Palace train station; Bus 2B,3,63,122,137,154,157,176,202, 227,249,351,358; **Entrance**: Free (entrance charge for farmyard); **Opening Times**: Daily, 7.30am-dusk; **Other Information**: Boating lake, bowling pitch, cafe, caravan club, children's playground, concert bowl, dogs welcome, dry ski slope, farm, maze, mini-railway, parking, sports centre, toilets; **Seasonal Features**: January, February, April, May, June, July, September, October, November, December; autumn tree colour, maze

Crystal Palace Park reminds us of the extravagance of the Victorians at its most extreme as well as providing a huge scale family park with panoramic views of town and country and year-round attractions for sportsman, plantsman and toddler alike. The 200 acre landscaped grounds provided a spectacular setting for Sir Joseph Paxton's vast Crystal Palace from 1854 until it burnt down in an immense inferno in 1936. Edward Milner and George Eyles originally designed the grounds with grand terraces, lakes, statues and formal flower beds. Since the fire, however, these have declined and it was only in 1960, when a large National Sports Centre was built in the park, that Bromley Council started a restoration programme. Today you can amble round a maze, a large boating lake with a life-size dinosaur trail, a farm, a fishing lake with waterlilies and the site of the old Crystal Palace with sphinxes and terraces still intact. There is also a walled garden on the hilltop and formal flower beds at all the main entrances as well as many mature trees which give an attractive display of autumn colours.

Standing today where the famous Exhibition Centre once stood you can join the huge stone sphinxes and dilapidated statues as they gaze from their pedestals over south-west London. It takes a while to appreciate the seemingly endless balustrades that front the terraces, now home to old ravens and tangled bindweed and brambles. If you leave the decaying grandeur to the buddleia and other scrub and head down to the modern National Sports Centre you will pass a large football stadium, dry ski slope, bowling pitch and cricket pitch among much else. Also in the south of the park lies the boating lake built in 1854 and famous for its collection of prehistoric monsters.

Crystal Palace Park contains London's largest maze, a circular tea maze constructed of hornbeam hedges surrounded by a crescent of Lombardy poplars and rhododendrons. This has recently been renovated by Bromley Council. Adjacent to the maze lies an area with good acoustics known as the Concert Bowl where concerts and firework displays take place next to a waterlily pond. A statue of Dante from the old Palace now guards an old terrace wall. Some mature trees in this area include Corsican pines, cork oak, turkey oak, strawberry tree and a huge sweet chestnut. In spring a stand of cherry trees is covered in blossom and in autumn many old oaks, young maples and silver birches put on a fiery display.

For the children, there are two children's playgrounds, a farm and a mini-railway to be investigated – not to mention the prehistoric monsters. For the plantsman there is a walled garden with spring-flowering azaleas and rhododendrons and more fine trees including a 300 year old English oak and tall avenue of London planes by the Penge entrance cafe. Crystal Palace Park does not contain many garden areas, but it is an interesting place to explore with space and attractions for all the family.

DULWICH PARK

Address: Dulwich Park, London SE21; Tel: 020 8693 5737; **Owner**: Southwark Borough Council; **Transport**: West & North Dulwich train stations; Bus 185,P13,P4; **Entrance**: Free; **Opening Times**: Daily, 8am-dusk (9pm May-Aug); **Other Information**: Bird walks, boating lake, café, disabled access (park map in Braille), dogs welcome, nature trails, tennis courts, toilets; **Seasonal Features**: April, May, June; azaleas, dry garden, Japanese garden, pondside gardens, rhododendrons, wild flowers

Dulwich Park is one of the best examples of the Victorian park as an idealized piece of countryside in a suburban environment. It was intended to offer a safe and relaxed atmosphere where visitors could get close to nature and this is still very much the case today, particularly if you partake in one of the early morning bird walks laid on by the park rangers.

In 1883, 29 hectares of land were given to the Metropolitan Board of Works by the now extensive Dulwich College on condition that it was made a public park. Several years later the new Dulwich Park was opened with 22 full-time gardeners, a large man-made lake and a fashionable rhododendron garden to which Queen Mary was a frequent visitor. The gate by which she entered the park was renamed in her honour.

Today the park has expanded to 72 acres and funding is being sought from the Lottery to improve visitor facilities. Geometrical flowerbeds have given way to less formal herbaceous borders and a wildlife area, dry garden and Japanese garden can all be found near the central boating lake. The rhododendrons and azaleas at the eastern end of the park are still impressive in spring and there are plans to extend the season by replacing 50% of the *Rhododendron ponticum* with different varieties. For the more energetic visitors the park has a private firm hiring bikes as well as many tennis courts and a large playground. For the more sedentary, an entrancing sculpture, the 'Divided Circle' by Barbara Hepworth can be found between the silver birches and weeping willows on the lakeside.

Dulwich Park is Grade 2 listed and, with Dulwich Common and Sydenham Hill Woods to its south, it still provides one of South London's most valued green spaces and wildlife havens.

EAST HAM NATURE RESERVE

Address: Norman Road, East Ham, London E6; **Tel**: 020 8470 4525; **Owner**: managed by Newham Parks & Conservation Services; **Transport**: East Ham tube (District Line); Beckton DLR station; Bus 101,104,300; **Entrance**: Free; **Opening Times**: Tue-Fri

10am-5pm, summer weekends 2-5pm, winter weekends 1-4pm; **Other Information**: Disabled access, no dogs, parking, toilets, visitor centre/classroom; **Seasonal Features**: April, May, July; daffodils, cowparsley, rosebay willowherb, summer meadow, wild flowers, woodland

The parish church of St Mary Magdalene is over 800 years old and is the only complete Norman building in the London postal district which was built as a parish church and is still used as such today. Its rambling churchyard is one of the largest in the country and, although there are no further burials here now, it is well managed as a local authority nature reserve and is home to many wild plants and animals.

Nature trails and woodland walks lie quietly waiting to be explored, paths are well marked with one trail specially adapted for wheelchairs, pushchairs and the use of white sticks. In March and April daffodils that through the years have been cast off old graves bloom, and these are followed by hawthorn, bluebells and fragrant viburnum which blossom near the church and visitor centre. In July the tall-growing rose-bay willow-herb provides an ocean of purple in the grassland along the eastern edge of the reserve. The other habitats here are woodland, hedge, scrub and meadow. The trees with interesting autumnal colours are silver birches, field maples, acers and rowans.

The area directly around the church is well mown so you can appreciate the building itself and species diversity is encouraged. The 12th century church consisted only of sanctuary, chancel and nave. The tower, south porch and west door were added later. The woodland is quiet and atmospheric and the grassland, scrub and meadow are spacious and restful places to look at the wild flowers or sit and watch the wildlife. The graveyard also contains some surprises, including several memorials to members of the crew of the Titanic and as you wander around the reserve you see many dilapidated graves with no one to care for them other than the ever-present dark ivy tentacles.

ELTHAM PALACE GARDEN

Address: Court Road, Eltham, London SE9; **Tel**: 020 8294 2548; **Owner**: English Heritage; **Transport**: Eltham or Mottingham train stations; Bus 126,131,161; **Entrance**: Entrance charge; **Opening Times**: Wed-Fri, Sun & Bank Hols, Nov-Mar 10am-4pm, Apr-Sep 10am-6pm, Oct 10am-5pm; **Other Information**: Cafe, no dogs, parking, shop, toilets; **Seasonal Features**: March, April, May, June, July,

Eltham Palace Garden

August; spring bulbs, wisteria, rose garden, rockery, herbaceous borders, roses, woodland gardens

Travel to Eltham Palace in south east London and you will leave the present and travel back to two distinct eras whose styles are subtly interwoven in house and garden. Substantial remains of an important medieval Royal Palace lie partially exposed in a particularly rare example of a well designed 1930's garden. Eltham was initially a moated manor house but became a palace when it was purchased by the royal family in 1305. The Palace was a favourite of Henry VIII and in the 16th century it was one of only six palaces large enough to accommodate and feed the entire court of 800 or more people. In the 17th century Eltham lost favour, however, and fell into decline to be used only by local farmers. In 1930 the ruined Palace and its grounds were bought by a rich and fashionable couple, Stephen and Virginia Courtauld, who had made their money in the manufacture of rayon. They were keen gardeners and top-class architects worked around the medieval remains to design a building with lavish decor, ultra-modern technology and impressive gardens for entertaining. The Courtaulds left Eltham in 1944 and until 1992 the Army Educational Corps was in residence. English Heritage is now in charge and a major restoration programme of the 1930's Eltham Palace interiors and gardens has almost been completed.

As you roam the grounds from exotic rockery to gnarled wisteria, you will find an entire 15th century stone bridge traversing the moat and excavated remains of Tudor royal apartments. Although the Courtaulds' twentieth century house with curved colonnade and staircase pavilions takes centre stage here now, the medieval jewel is Edward IV's Great Hall, erected in the 1470's as a dining hall for the court. There are mature trees including a strawberry tree with clusters of bright fruit in autumn, a bay laurel, Indian bean tree and walnut tree on the lawn and a fine magnolia leaning on the Great Hall. The Courtaulds put in a sunken rose garden which has been replanted with rose cultivars popular in the 1930's – including hybrid teas and fragrant hybrid musks. It flowers in June/July and is adjacent to several gardens of year round colour featuring snowdrops, hellebores, hydrangeas, viburnum and anemones.

Other typical 1930 features include a well maintained rock garden sited along the eastern moat bank. It is planted with various Japanese trees, shrubs and herbs with a series of pools and waterfalls. The south moat is now dry and covered in lawn which is crossed by a 1930's oak bridge supported by medieval brick and stone foundations. The moat bank here is ablaze with spring flowers, especially daffodils, from March to May. A recently redesigned, 100m-long, mixed herbaceous border along the lawn encompasses the whole colour spectrum from spring to autumn.

Eltham Palace Gardens probably reach their peak each year in June and July when the roses and the majority of other plants are flowering. However, this is a garden holding colour, foliage and fragrance throughout the year and there is always the house to see with its sumptuous art-deco interior.

EMSLIE HORNIMAN PLEASANCE PARK

Address: East Row, London W10; **Tel**: 020 7602 9483 **Owner**: North Kensington Council; **Location**: Between East Row & Bosworth Rd, North Kensington; **Transport**: Westbourne Park tube (Hamm. & City Line); Bus 23,52,70,295,302; **Entrance**: Free; **Opening Times**: Daily, 8.30am-dusk; **Other Information**: Cafe, children's playground, dogs welcome, multi sports pitch, toilets; **Seasonal Features**: June, July, August; herbaceous border with stream and oak bridge, pergola

Emslie Horniman Pleasance Park is an attractive garden and park hidden away in North Kensington which since 1998 has undergone remarkable reconstruction. In 1913-14 it was designed as a Spanish garden by C. Voysey, a well known Arts and Crafts architect. However it was badly neglected over the years and only in the 1990's was money raised through the National Lottery to fund stylish renovation work for the community.

The original Spanish style bridge has been completely reconstructed in English oak along with the massive pergolas up which roses and clematis now scramble. The original planting schemes of Voysey inspired the landscape designer Jane Fearnley-Whittingstall, who supervised all the garden's replanting. The flower beds running along the centre are designed for a long flowering season; they display a mixture of bright colours and soft and decorative foliage. August comes ablaze with sunflowers, marigolds, rudbeckia, echinops and clumps of lavender. Purple and yellow tend to predominate in mid summer and for those who want to sit and relax the central flower bed is the more informal and easy on the eye, while the encircling stream gently supports waterlilies and damselflies.

Surrounding and sheltering the peaceful garden is a whitewashed wall with turrets and more plant beds which help you forget the outside world as you sit enjoying the profusion of scent and colour inside.

FENTON HOUSE GARDEN

Address: Hampstead Grove, London NW3; **Tel**: 020 7435 3471; **Owner**: The National Trust; **Transport**: Hampstead Tube; Bus 46,268; **Entrance**: Entrance charge; **Opening Times**: 6 Mar-4 April Sat-Sun 2-5pm; 7 April-31 Oct Sat, Sun & Bank Hols Mon 11am-5pm; Wed, Thurs & Fri 2-5pm; last admission 30 mins before closing. Closed Mon & Tues; **Other Information**: Disabled access, no dogs or picnics allowed, toilets in house; **Seasonal Features**: March, April, May, June, July, September, October, November, December; anemones, daffodils, fritillaries, fruit blossom, herbs, orchard, parterre, rose garden, vegetable garden, herbaceous borders, standard hollies, yew topiary

Fenton House is perched high up in Hampstead on a pleasant road just to the west of Hampstead Heath. It is a bold late 17th century mansion with detailed brickwork and its surrounding walled garden, though only one acre in size, contains some well established sections which give it a succinct charm and allure to draw you in.

As you wander through the neatly trimmed yew hedges you will encounter a beautiful display of asters, lavenders, and other colourful and aromatic plants; fragrances are captured in the still air and benches provide a quiet resting spot. There is also a grassy orchard with 30 different varieties of apple, a spring-flowering herbaceous border and enchanting spring bulbs such as fritillaries, primroses, anemones and narcissi. A well-established, sheltered rose garden blossoms in June and July when a 60-metre summer herbaceous border stocked with delphiniums, lupins and lilies is also worth viewing. Clematis, wisteria and magnolia snake up the old walls providing summer-long colour and, on a clear day, you are treated to stunning panoramic views of the City from the raised border path.

Fenton House itself surveys a fine lawn and a regimental row of tubs with standard-trained variegated holly (*Ilex* 'Silver Queen'). On its opposite side stands a beautiful set of Tijou-designed wrought-iron gates which can be reached via a robinia avenue from the formal south garden. Its small vegetable garden includes a plot of flowers that are grown for the indoor cut flower arrangements. Fenton House Garden is quietly impressive and provides you with a sense of freshness, age and beauty.

FULHAM PALACE PARK   *See illustration 16, between pages 96 and 97*

Address: Bishops Avenue, Fulham Palace Road, London SW6; **Tel**: 020 7736 3233; **Owner**: London Borough of Hammersmith and Fulham; **Transport**: Putney Bridge tube (District Line); Bus 14,74,220; **Entrance**: Free; **Opening Times**: Daily, except

25 Dec & 1 Jan, 8am-dusk; **Other Information**: Disabled access, dogs welcome, garden centre at entrance gate, museum in Palace, tours every 2nd Sun of the month at 2pm; **Seasonal Features**: April, May, June, July, September, October; cherry blossom, magnolias, wisteria, Judas tree, orchard, herb garden, autumnal trees

Leave behind the modern day bustle of Fulham Palace Road and, after passing the busy garden centre and tennis courts, you leave behind hundreds of years of history and enter the beautiful, spacious 41 acre park and garden surrounding Fulham Palace. From the 11th century until 1973, the Palace was the abode of the Bishops of London and one of them, Henry Compton, Bishop of London 1675-1713, was a very keen plantsman. He was responsible for the introduction of many rare plants and people came from all over England to see them in his garden.

One of the present day treasures of Fulham Palace grounds is the flowering of the wisteria in April and May. There is a magnificent old wisteria pergola in the walled garden and a climbing wisteria on the south side of the Palace. Another feature that should not be missed is the tree collection, for which maps are provided in the museum situated in the Palace itself. On the Great Lawn, trees older than 150 years include the Judas tree, beautiful in spring, the great blue Atlas cedar and the contorted sweet chestnut. The Cedar of Lebanon found opposite the museum entrance was planted in the 18th century.

At the eastern end of the lawn a fine Tudor Gate overlooks a somewhat larger than expected 19th century knot garden. Inside you will find a mixture of old greenhouses, neatly planted aromatic herb gardens, bay trees, and the wonderful wisteria, at least 100 years old. During the 1970's the Council increased the walled garden by planting new order beds and adding to the existing orchard with some old varieties of fruit trees.

Adjacent to the gardens is Bishop's Park which was developed on land along the riverside presented to the people of Fulham by the Bishop of London in the 19th century. An embankment was built to prevent flooding of the public park and the Victorians planted it with a fine avenue of London plane trees. These remain today and you can walk at will round the park, though it is not nearly as colourful or relaxing as Fulham Palace Gardens.

GEFFRYE MUSEUM GARDENS

Address: Kingsland Road, London E2; **Tel**: 020 7739 9893; **Owner**: Geffrye Museum; **Transport**: Liverpool Street tube (Central, Circle & Metropolitan Lines); Bus 22A,22B,67,149,243; **Entrance**: Free; **Opening Times**: 1 April-31 Oct; daily, except Monday (open Bank Hols.), Tue-Sat 10am-5pm, Sun 12-5pm; **Other Information**: Cafe in museum, disabled access, guide dogs only, events, museum open all year (same hours as garden – free admission), shop, toilets; **Seasonal Features**: June, July, August, September, October; herb garden, period gardens, hydrangeas

In the middle of Hackney in the East End lie some charming and well tended gardens with an historical interest to rival any in the capital. They belong to the Geffrye Museum which is an attractive 18th-century building – the former almshouses of the Ironmonger's Company. Today it contains a fascinating display of English furniture in period settings as well as a good quality modern cafe, and is well worth a visit.

The front gardens comprise a sweeping, formal lawn overhung by large London plane trees and bordered by lengthy beds planted with hydrangeas, hostas and brightly coloured pelargoniums. Virginia creeper trails up the Georgian museum facade, turning a rich crimson in autumn. Behind the museum you will discover some more recent garden developments – a small, walled herb garden is an oasis of scent and quiet and there is an interesting display of period gardens portray changing horticultural styles from early Elizabethan to Edwardian.

The herb garden has three arbours where you can rest under pale climbing roses and jasmine. Lavender beds bloom abundantly in summer around a central ceramic fountain and an aromatic bed is filled with muskmallow, rosemary and florentine iris. Bee plants, dye plants and culinary, cosmetic and medicinal herbs are all given separate beds with plants clearly labelled and some rare species included. Though small, this garden is sheltered and quiet and you are encouraged to rub some plants to release the scent.

The period gardens show garden plots such as may have been seen in towns from the 16th century through to the Edwardian era. There are four plots in all: Elizabethan, Georgian, Victorian and Edwardian. For each area there is an informative panel with key plants and design features clearly marked. It is interesting to see the progression in garden design so clearly displayed, and time spent wandering through the Geffrye Museum Gardens is fun and informative as well as peaceful and relaxing.

GOLDERS GREEN CREMATORIUM, GARDENS OF REMEMBRANCE

Address: 62 Hoop Lane, Golders Green, London NW11; **Tel**: 020 8455 2374; **Owner**: London Cremation Company plc; **Transport**: Golders Green tube (Northern Line); Bus 82,120,260,H2; **Entrance**: Free (no organized groups); **Opening Times**: Daily, summer 9am-6pm, winter 9am-4pm, Chapel of Memory 9am-4pm; **Other Information**: Café, car parking, disabled access, guide dogs only, toilets; **Seasonal Features**: March, April, May, June, September, October; alpine garden, crocuses, daffodils, maples, rhododendrons, roses, tulips

Here is indeed a real gem of a garden, peaceful, colourful, atmospheric, spacious and beautifully maintained. It is, in fact, the first, and currently, the only crematorium garden to be listed by English Heritage and is a treat to visit for all its horticultural, architectural and commemorative value.

Prior to 1885 cremation was illegal in this country. Since then, however, demand for the practice grew steadily and by 1902 it had become necessary to establish a crematorium within easy reach of central London. Golders Green Crematorium was then founded by the late Sir Henry Thompson and is now recognized as the world's foremost crematorium. All religions are included and a Jewish shrine in the grounds is the only specially designated area. A list of some of the more well-known people whose ashes lie there is available from the office and includes Marc Bolan, Sigmund Freud, Anna Pavlova and Paul Kossof whose memorial bears his words, "all right now".

The ornate red brick crematorium comprises a large columbarium with a pavilion tower at either end, and 4 chapels, of which the Chapel of Memory is open for quiet prayer. Extensive rose beds and a lily pond line the crematorium cloisters and each rose, like every plant in the garden, is a memorial to someone and is labelled accordingly. The garden takes the form of a large, central lawn, used as a dispersal area, with colourful, leafy avenues running up each side. At the far end are more roses, a tranquil cedar lawn and the beautifully kept Horder Garden with ponds, alpines and a copse. Heather, almond, rhododendron, berberis and acer collections grace visitors with their seasonal blooms while numerous mixed herbaceous beds, shrubberies and a woodland glade provide year round interest. The roses flower up to September but most spectacular are the 2-3 million crocuses that flood the central dispersal lawn with colour each spring. Understandably visitors come quite some distance to see such a fine display and, as the crocuses are under-planted with daffodils and tulips, the show continues through from February to April.

As you amble thoughtfully around such an atmospheric and pleasing garden, you will discover the Phillipson Mausoleum, designed by Edward Lutyens, as well as the secluded Children's Garden of Remembrance. Seats are plentiful and a visit to this immaculately kept eden of flowers and memories is not easily forgotten.

GOLDERS HILL PARK

Address: North End Way, Hampstead, London NW3; **Tel**: 020 8455 5183; **Owner**: Corporation of London; **Transport**: Golders Green tube (Northern Line); Bus 210,268; **Entrance**: Free; **Opening Times**: Daily 7.30am-dusk; **Other Information**: Cafe (March-October in Park), disabled access, dogs welcome, events, plant sales, no barbecues on Heath, toilets; **Seasonal Features**: May, June, July; formal bedding, dahlias and herbaceous borders in flower garden, azaleas, rhododendrons and primulas in water garden

Golders Hill Park is a remarkably well maintained 36-acre public park on the western side of Hampstead Heath with rolling lawns, an interesting collection of trees, a colourful, well-stocked flower garden and a recently developed water garden featuring azaleas, rhododendrons and primulas in spring. In summer the walled flower garden and pond area contains some of the most colourful annual bedding to be found in any public London park, as well as palms, magnolias, bananas and a eucalyptus. There is an attractive pergola swathed in clematis and a large dahlia bed which blooms in August and September after the cannas, petunias, marigolds and lobelias, etc.

Elsewhere in the park you can entertain the children at the zoo or walk up Golders Hill to admire the view stretching south and west. Rhododendrons line the top of the hill and put on a welcome display in May and June when the formal bedding is also at its best. From here you can wander east into the wooded part of West Heath or stay in Golders Hill Park to see the ancient oaks, large sculpture, bamboos and leafy horse chestnut avenue leading to the tennis courts. In spring there is plenty of blossom with cherry trees, lilacs, laburnums and crab apples; and in autumn acers and old oaks take the stage.

For a final rest and recuperation the cafe is situated on the north east edge of the park by North End Road and has fabulous views of the City. Sitting amongst sweeping lawns, attractive hanging baskets, old, contorted, mulberry trees and a mature, well-rounded sweet chestnut you can really make the most of a cup of tea.

GRAY'S INN GARDENS

Address: Gray's Inn Road, London WC1; **Owner**: Gray's Inn; **Transport**: Chancery Lane tube (Central Line); Bus 17,19,38,45,46,55,171A,243,505; **Entrance**: Free; **Opening Times**: Mon-Fri, 12-2.30pm; **Other Information**: No dogs; **Seasonal Features**: April, May, June; cherry blossom, magnolias

These large, historic and somewhat empty gardens seem almost hallowed ground as they lie closely guarded by arboreal giants and the faceless windows of the Gray's Inn Court buildings. The restricted public opening hours explain the occasional lack of visitors to the gardens although if you do manage to enter through the iron gates you will find peace and space, with a good mixture of both young and very old trees. Many benches are provided and there is some attractive spring blossom to be seen in April and May with cherries, magnolias and hawthorns predominating.

The public entrance to the gardens is on Theobalds Road and an avenue of young oaks runs from here to the southernmost gate. The oldest trees are Indian bean trees which bear large flowers in July and keep their bean-like fruits all winter. There are also some ancient magnolia specimens and a large number of towering London planes. A well-kept lawn carpets the ground and terraces rise up to the north and west. The rest of the garden is designed for low maintenance and contains a large shrubbery and several small herbaceous borders which between them have a long flowering season and year-round structure.

These neat gardens seem a well-kept secret and the opening hours do, indeed, make it difficult for many to visit to them. They contain much history and are a haven from the pace of city life beyond their railings.

GREAT TREES OF LONDON

London is well known for its magnificent collection of trees, there are in fact over six million of them in the capital making an important stand against pollution and enriching our lives in ways we often take completely for granted. Trees for London has established an initiative whereby a handful of particularly important trees are nominated as 'Great Trees of London'. These may be very large have a peculiar shape or an interesting history or are of prime importance to wildlife. Registered trees can be identified by their green plaques and all are clearly visible to the public. The following are accessible by London Underground although for details of any 'Great Trees' in your area you should contact the Trees for London,

Prince Consort Lodge, Kennington Park, Kennington Park Place, London SE11 4AS, Tel: 020 7587 1320.

Wembley Elm (*Ulmus sp*) – a large landmark tree which may be 100 years old. Its good condition and form is unusual for an elm in London. Dutch Elm Disease has meant mature examples of this species are now comparatively rare throughout the country.

Location: corner of Harrow Road and Oakington Manor Drive, Wembley.

Transport: Wembley Central tube (Bakerloo Line), Wembley Park tubes (Metropolitan & Jubilee Lines)

The Barnsbury Beech (*Fagus sylvatica*) – a huge mature tree with twisting double trunks and wonderful autumn colours.

Location: outside Thornhill House, at the junction of Barnsbury Park and Thornhill Road.

Transport: Highbury & Islington tube (Victoria Line) and train station

Asgill House Copper Beech (*Fagus sylvatica*) – Planted during the late 18th century in the grounds of Asgill House. The tree is a noted feature of the Thames at Richmond.

Location: Asgill House, Old Palace Lane, Richmond – on the Thames towpath between Richmond Bridge and Twickenham Railway Bridge.

Transport: Richmond tube (District Line)

Black Horse Pollarded Chestnut (*Aesculus hippocastanum*) – a wide-spreading, multi-pollarded horse chestnut of extraordinary shape.

Location: in the car park/beer garden of the Black Horse pub, Queen's Road, Richmond

Transport: Richmond tube (District Line)

Morden Cemetery Horse Chestnut (*Aesculus hippocastanum*) – Two trees have merged to form a single canopy with branches sweeping down to the ground. An unusual, attractive and distinctive feature.

Location: by the Garden of Remembrance, Morden Cemetery, Morden.

Transport: Morden tube (Northern Line) then M1 bus

The Dorchester Plane (*Platanus × hispanica*) – a large semi-mature London plane with beautiful shape, very dramatic when lit up at night. A landmark for London's West End.

Location: outside the Dorchester, Park Lane, W1

Transport: Green Park & Hyde Park Corner tubes (Piccadilly & Victoria Lines)

GREENWICH ROYAL PARK   *See illustration 27, between pages 96 and 97*

Address: Greenwich Park, Blackheath Gate, London SE10; **Tel**: 020 8858 2608; **Owner**: The Royal Parks; **Transport**: Greenwich, Maze Hill, Blackheath train stations; Island Gardens DLR station; Bus 53, 177, 180, 286; Boats from Charing Cross Pier; **Entrance**: Free; **Opening Times**: Daily, dawn-dusk; **Other Information**: Cafe, dogs welcome, events, National Maritime Museum, Ranger's House, Royal Observatory, shop, sports facilities, toilets; **Seasonal Features**: April, May, June, July, August, September, October; spring bulbs, formal bedding, herbaceous border, rhododendrons, azaleas, herbs, rose garden, autumnal trees

For a botanical and historical treat of regal proportions you should head to Greenwich Royal Park on the south bank of the Thames and amble round flower gardens, Roman remains, royal palaces, historic tree avenues and the famous Royal Observatory on the Greenwich Meridian Line. For the plantsman there is a rose garden with no less than 113 different varieties, a herb garden, an historic tree collection and a large flower garden with a lake and some lovely autumnal foliage. The historian, meanwhile, can indulge in the Royal Observatory, Vanburgh Castle, the National Maritime Museum and the Ranger's House which contains the Suffolk Art Collection.

The handsome Palladian villa by St Mary's Gate was built by Inigo Jones in 1616 as the Queen's House. It was later a Royal Naval Hospital and now houses the National Maritime Museum. Its elegant promenades link the central stately villa to its grand wings added in the early 19th century. Statues of haughty figures pose proudly on the surrounding lawns and cannons sit threateningly by entrances. Nothing is scrimped on at Greenwich, flower borders seem wider, tree avenues longer and older and architecture and views more impressive than elsewhere. The longest herbaceous border in Greater London runs in front of the National Maritime Museum and brims with diverse colour and texture from May to September.

The Royal Observatory designed by Sir Christopher Wren perches on the hill east of St Mary's Gate and is reached via one of the many formal avenues of trees that were first laid out between September 1661 and June 1662. Rows of sweet chestnuts were planted, some of which still survive in Great Cross Avenue and Bower Avenue, from where you also get a stunning view of London on a clear day. Over 400 trees were destroyed in the park in the 1987 hurricane and Queen Elizabeth's Oak, in which the Virgin Queen was supposed to have sheltered, was lost in 1990. Nonetheless there are still 3,000 trees here including a notable collection of oaks, horse chestnuts and beeches and the autumnal colours, especially in the flower garden, are remarkable.

Just to the south of St Mary's Gate lies a scented herb garden. It is at its most fragrant in June and July when the majority of its 32 different types of herbs are flowering. These range from balm and catmint to thyme and woodruff and include rosemary, which was the favourite herb of the Elizabethans . Also reaching its peak in mid summer is the large rose garden overlooked by the Ranger's House which is a red brick, 18th century mansion housing the Suffolk Collection of portraits and musical instruments. Well-maintained and labelled, the rose garden is both colourful and extensive and a gracious beech and cedar of Lebanon add to its formality.

At the southern end of Greenwich Park lies an exotic and beautiful flower garden while a sunken rhododendron dell hides under a huge beech tree by Blackheath Gate. The dell is a blaze of colour in April and May and full of birdlife. The flower garden contains over thirty flower beds with startling displays of spring bulbs, bedding plants and perennials all punctuated by sweeping cedars and an exotic range of broadleaf trees. It is secluded and peaceful and a large paper-bark birch, a Judas tree, magnolias, azaleas, ginkgos, maples and a heather bed give much seasonal colour. A sunken lake with small fountain is popular with families and there is a nearby cafe and wilderness area with a herd of deer.

With a children's playground at the northern end, tennis courts by the Ranger's House and cricket, rugby and hockey to watch in season, one is not stuck for activities in Greenwich Park. There are also two cafes and a bandstand where concerts are regularly held in summer. Visiting the park today, walking up 340 year old tree-lined avenues and viewing Wren's and Inigo Jones' classical masterpieces, as well as the remains of a Romano-Celtic temple possibly from the 2nd century AD, can be an enriching experience. The gardens are worth the trip from spring to autumn and the views are admirable.

GUNNERSBURY PARK *See illustration 15, between pages 96 and 97*

Address: Popes Lane, London W3; **Tel**: 020 8992 1612; **Owner**: London Boroughs of Ealing and Hounslow; **Transport**: Acton Town tube (District & Piccadilly Lines); Bus E3, H91; **Entrance**: Free; **Opening Times**: Daily, 8 am-dusk; **Other Information**: Arts centre, boating pond, cafe, car park, children's playground, disabled access, dogs welcome, events, fishing pond, museum for the London boroughs of Ealing & Hounslow – free admission, sports facilities, toilets; **Seasonal Features**: March, April, September, October; daffodils, autumnal trees

Gunnersbury Park contains a spacious 186 acres of old parkland encompassing two mansions, pockets of woodland, a hidden lake and some majestic specimen trees. It once formed a private estate last owned by the Rothschild family who transformed the design of the grounds under the guidance of the architect, Sidney Smirke. In the 1920's the London boroughs of Ealing & Hounslow bought the estate from Leopold de Rothschild and in 1926 Gunnersbury opened as a public park.

Two Neoclassical mansions in the north east of the park stand atop rolling lawns containing a rockery, roses and an elegant orangery. Built as private residences in the 19th century these now contain a museum, Victorian kitchens and an arts centre. Nearby, a large round pond, thought to have been designed by William Kent, is overlooked by a handsome temple and formal rose garden. The pond is now a boating lake with an adjacent cafe and a poet's corner shelters beneath cedars by the temple. A shrubbery planted for year round interest leads from the pond to a large children's playground and an area of numerous sports facilities covers the old parkland. Some of the old estate farm buildings still stand at the heart of the sprawling park and serve as today as changing rooms and an out-door snackbar.

Beside the smaller of the two mansions sits an 18th century bath house which is currently being restored, while the remains of some Japanese gardens can be found behind the old stables. In the south west corner of the park lies a deep pond known as the Potomac which is a popular fishing lake. Well hidden amongst mature trees and evergreens this is home to many birds and on its banks lurks a desolate three-storeyed gothic tower which acted as a boathouse-cum-bell tower when it was first built in the 1860's.

Ham House

Gunnersbury Park has several interesting and well-labelled buildings and features documenting its chequered history. It contains many spectacular trees, some of which are particularly rare or richly coloured in autumn, such as the Japanese maple, keaki, sweet gum and pin oak. A beautiful fern-leaved beech near the orangery is one of the most impressive specimen trees. In spring, daffodils bloom along the avenue of mature plane trees leading along the south eastern park wall while elsewhere, cherry, plums and hawthorns all blossom abundantly.

HAM HOUSE
See illustration 26, between pages 96 and 97

Address: Ham Street, Richmond, Surrey TW10; **Tel**: 020 8940 1950; **Owner**: The National Trust; **Location**: On the south bank of the Thames west of Richmond Park; **Transport**: Richmond tube (District Line) & train station; Bus 65,371; **Entrance**: Entrance charge; **Opening Times**: Gardens open Sat-Wed 11am-6pm (or dusk if earlier); House open Easter to Oct, Sat-Wed 1-5pm; **Other Information**: Disabled access, no dogs, events, restaurant, shop, toilets; **Seasonal Features**: April, May, June; old english garden, parterre, roses, herbaceous borders, herbs, peonies, lavender, wild flowers

Ham House is an imposing Jacobean residence built in a fashionable Thameside district in 1610 for Sir Thomas Vavasour. It was inherited later that century by Elizabeth Dysart, an ambitious lady with a taste for luxury who spent vast sums on refining her home and garden. To impress the many visitors the rolling grounds were formally laid out with avenues, parterres, orangeries and fountains with styles adopted from France, Holland and Italy. The Dysart family owned Ham House until 1948 when it was given over to the National Trust and there is currently an on-going restoration programme to return the gardens to their 17th century glory.

As you approach the great house from the river, walking up a tree-lined avenue and through the main gateway, the building and accompanying statues silently welcome you as they boldly stand amidst the rambling grounds. To the east of the house is the peaceful cherry garden in 1682 contained beds of fashionable plants such as jasmine, gillyflowers and hollyhocks surrounded by 40 morello cherry trees. The garden was restored in 1975 and an arbour of pleached hornbeams now encircles fragrant beds of santolina and lavender. There is also a marble statue of Bacchus.

To provide ladies with a convenient area in which to promenade, a terrace was built along the south side of the house with stunning views up Richmond Hill. Paths were lined by aromatic and exotic plants in fancy tubs – there were 152 in 1682. Today a single border runs along the South Terrace containing a formal 17th century flower bed with fan-trained plums and a pomegranate. Below the terrace are eight neatly mown grass squares with tubs, aromatics and topiary shrubs.

In contrast to the formal terraces and lawns is an area known as the wilderness. This was a horticultural feature popular in the 17th century in which wild flowers and meadow grass were cultivated in a geometrical arrangement of clipped hedges. The central park was originally lined with statues as can be seen from a painting of the house dated 1675 and this arrangement is being restored by the National Trust. The wilderness was, and still is, a place where you could find both privacy within the hedged compartments and relaxation amidst the natural meadow flora. It is an ideal place to escape from the cares of everyday life and one can also find refreshment in the attractive orangery. This is rumoured to be the oldest orangery in the country, built around 1670, and is situated in the newly restored 17th century kitchen garden.

HAMPTON COURT PALACE
GARDENS

See illustration 24, between pagesg 96 and 97

Address: East Molesey, Surrey KT8; **Tel**: 0870 752 7777; **Owner**: Historic Royal Palaces Trust; **Location**: North side of Hampton Court bridge; **Transport**: Hampton Court train station; Bus 111,216,411,416,451,461,513,726,R68; **Entrance**: Rose garden, wilderness & east front gardens – all free; maze, privy garden, sunken garden & Great Vine – entrance charge; **Opening Times**: Daily, dawn-dusk (maze & privy garden, Oct-Mar 9.30am-4.30pm, Mon 10.15am-4.30pm;Apr-Sept 9.30am-6pm). Closed 24-26 Dec; **Other Information**: Disabled access, dogs on leads only, events, parking, picnic area, restaurants, shops, toilets; **Seasonal Features**: January, February, March, April, May, June, July, August, September, November, December; cherry blossom, daffodils, laburnum, knot garden, rose garden, formal bedding, tulips, herbaceous borders, pondside garden, Great Vine, privy garden, topiary, maze

Hampton Court Palace has stood majestically alongside the Thames for over 500 years. Six acres of buildings crowned with numerous turrets, chimneys and spires are set amidst sixty acres of beautifully landscaped riverside gardens which are themselves enveloped in six hundred acres of rolling deer park. The visitor certainly has much to explore and all ages and tastes are well catered for throughout the year.

The maze was planted in 1690 for William of Orange and is now visited by approximately 330,000 people every year – most find their way out again! It is located just inside the impressive Lion Gates and has some interesting trees and bedding displays nearby- all worth seeing in the winter months. In the spring the whole of the surrounding area comes alive with blossom. The stars of this floral display are daffodils, cherry blossom, camellias and the laburnum walk which puts on a show of immense proportions.

Another part of the garden not to be missed in spring is the delicate, intriguingly beautiful privy garden to the south of the Palace. This was laid out in 1702 for William III as his private garden and was specially designed to complement Sir Christopher Wren's King's apartments. It subsequently underwent many changes but in 1995 as much as possible was restored and now the original 17th century architectural features, parterres, topiary and spring and summer displays of plants are so finely balanced you feel you could have been transported back 300 years. The planting has taken place on a grand scale and no less than 30,000 box plants line the delicate Baroque style flower beds. In spring these sparkle with crocuses, primroses, tulips, violets, narcissus and hyacinthus and in summer they come alive with blue cornflowers, coneflowers, marigolds, snap dragons, roses, lavender, honeysuckle, senecio and dianthus. The beds are punctuated by round headed variegated hollies and pyramidal yews and on the western terrace of the garden is Queen Mary's Bower, a spectacular 5.5 metres high and 100 metres long. This is a beautiful oak bower covered over now with a total of 296 trained hornbeam trees. If you walk to the far end of the privy garden you have a wonderful view of the Thames and the Palace and you can also see the majestic Tijou Screen. This consists of the original 12 wrought iron panels from King William's garden of 1702 and was made by the King's favoured wrought iron craftsman, the Frenchman Jean Tijou.

Also to the south of the Palace are the pond gardens where, in Tudor times, fish were bred and stocked for the Palace kitchens. Now there are a series of small, enclosed gardens, one sunken and still with a central pond, and the others walled with borders of exotics and colourful perennials. The sunken garden contains three tiers of colourful bedding plants, and is surrounded on three sides by pleached hornbeam underplanted with wisteria. A handsome Banqueting House built and finely decorated for King William sits squarely in this part of the garden as does the lower orangery where the Mantegna cartoons 'The Triumphs of Caesar' are on display.

There is one final surprise hidden between the Palace and the river – the oldest known vine in the world. It was planted here in 1768 by the then head gardener Lancelot 'Capability' Brown and today spreads into every permitted crevice in its vine glasshouse and has formed an incredibly vast stem. In 1795 a crop of some 1,499 bunches of grapes was reportedly harvested from it and today it yields an average of 500 to 700 bunches per year. The Great Vine, as it is known, has very fragrant small flowers which bloom in May and steadily form the sweet black grapes harvested over three weeks in September.

The largest, most spacious, section of Hampton Court Palace Gardens is the great fountain garden which lies to the east of the Palace and looks onto the 568 acre Home Park. A broad central path runs along the front of the Palace and is edged by what some describe as the longest herbaceous border in the country. Along the other paths which radiate from the Palace's east front entrance are rectangular flower beds full of tulips and summer bedding, bold hieroglyphs of colour against the green lawns. Also standing in regimental rows are avenues of limes, neatly trimmed hollies and large, pyramidal yews. A central pond makes a relaxing place to sit and to take in some of the surrounding splendour or you may choose to wander round the semi-circular canal that divides the fountain garden from Home Park and was dug for Queen Anne in 1710-1711.

A more recent feature the 20th century garden which was set up in 1984 as an arboretum and apprentice training garden. In contrast to much of the Tudor and Baroque style gardens this is an informal, more naturalistic area and is lovely to visit on a sultry spring or summer day, since it contains many aromatic herbs. Heathers, tree heathers and fuchsias all flower here in mid summer under some rare trees which are all labelled .

Hampton Court Gardens also include a huge walled rose garden with a collection of graceful statues which is lovely in June and July. The adjacent walled gardens, which were once Henry VIII's old jousting and archery grounds, are clad in wisteria and clematis which bloom for most of the summer. Some grand old trees can be found such as liquidambars, copper beeches, blue atlas cedars and large dawn redwoods. Elsewhere large and bright herbaceous borders steal the show with nerine lilies, sunflowers, acanthus, alliums and gladioli. A cafe nestles by the rose garden and some sustenance is gratefully received as there is much to see and a lot of ground to be covered during a visit to this palatial garden.

HILL GARDEN   *See illustration 13, between pages 32 and 33*

Address: Inverforth Close, North End Way, London NW3; **Tel**: 020 8455 5183; **Owner**: Corporation of London; **Location**: Inverforth House, Hampstead; **Transport**: Golders Green tube (Northern Line); Bus 210, H2; **Entrance**: Free; **Opening Times**: 8.30am-1hr before sunset; **Other Information**: No dogs; **Seasonal Features**: April, May, June, July, September, October; clematis, honeysuckles, lily pond, wisteria, rhododendrons

To find a secret garden on a grandiose scale you should head to the top of Hampstead Heath and seek out an unobtrusive little back alley that runs down the side of Inverforth House which is situated on North End Way. This large mansion used to be Lord Leverhulme's house, known as The Hill, and it was he who had the garden designer Thomas Mawson draw up plans for the spectacle that confronts you as you reach the back of his former residence.

The garden is today dominated by a massive Edwardian pergola which was built between 1906 and 1925 and comprises stone balustrades and pillars snaking in all directions to domed rose temples. The pergola is mounted on high walls which originally concealed potting sheds, etc., and the covered, raised walks offer stunning views across to Harrow-on-the-Hill. Designed to screen the house from Hampstead Heath and to look as extravagant as possible without obstructing the view of the Hill, the venerable, raised pergola is now cloaked in gnarled climbers of remarkable age and structure. Spring, summer and autumn are all colourful times to visit the garden, with fruit blossom, climbers, autumnal vines and fruits on the pergola and rhododendrons, azaleas and autumnal foliage on the heath below. There are also well kept formal gardens and lawns in front of Inverforth House.

At the base of the solid red brick wall bearing the pergola is a Mediterranean-style garden with gravel paths. It contains a mixture of pot-plants, beds and borders where bamboos, yuccas, rosemary, roses, acanthus, narcissi and alchemillas happily co-exist. The garden stretches the whole way along the base of the looming wall and climbing plants scale the brickwork between the decorative arches.

Once inside the towering pergola you will be amazed at the variety of shades, shapes and sizes of plants that twist themselves round the pillars and balustrades. There are luscious autumnal vines, variegated ivies, huge, ghostly wisterias, fragrant jasmines and entwining honeysuckles. Aged magnolias, long-flowering clematis, rambling roses and a spreading kiwi fruit are all very much at home on this lavish Edwardian construction which sweeps you proudly along on a scenic botanical journey. On one side you look down on the birch and rowan groves of West Heath which lead westwards through scrub vegetation to the Leg of Mutton Pond and eventually to Golders Hill Park. On your other side you can peer through the columns of the pergola to the formal gardens with sweeping lawns, grand trees, herbaceous borders and a central lily pond in front of Inverforth House. Within the pergola at this innermost spot are planted herbs in raised beds and some exotic climbers.

The Hill Garden also has a mystique due to its age and sense of decaying grandeur that is quite special. There has recently been a £2 million reconstruction project undertaken on the garden which has saved the pergola but luckily left the magic intact.

HOLLAND PARK See illustration 12, between pages 32 and 33

Address: Kensington, London W8; **Tel**: 020 7602 9483; **Owner**: Royal Borough of Kensington and Chelsea; **Location**: Between Holland Park Avenue & Kensington High Street; **Transport**: High Street Kensington tube (District Line); Kensington (Olympia) train station; Bus 9,9A,10,27,28,49,94; **Entrance**: Free; **Opening Times**: Daily, 7.30am-dusk; **Other Information**: Dogs welcome in restricted areas, parking, restaurant, teas, toilets; **Seasonal Features**: April, May, June, July, September; formal bedding, camellias, snowdrop tree, iris garden, azaleas, roses, dahlias, Japanese garden

Sandwiched between the major arterial routes of Kensington High Street and Holland Park Avenue, Holland Park is a green oasis that serves as both somewhat of a surprise and a great relief. In its relatively small area, about 54 acres, you can wander peacefully round a Dutch garden, an azalea walk, a woodland enclosure, the well manicured Kyoto garden, a dahlia garden and an iris garden. There is also a lovely old orangery where art exhibitions are held during the summer months. Much of the famous Holland House was destroyed in World War II but the formal gardens created in 1812 have been maintained and embellished. There are now excellent children's facilities and peacocks can be found strutting around the various lawns. Serious plantsmen can indulge in rare trees such as the pyrean oak, Chinese sweet gum, violet willow, Himalayan birch and the snowdrop tree which flowers in May.

The Kyoto garden, an oasis donated by the Japanese in 1991, is particularly peaceful and neat. Many tastes are catered for in Holland Park, with colour from early spring to late summer provided by bedding plants, azaleas, rhododendrons, spring flowers, camellias, roses, irises and dahlias. There are stately avenues of trees for walkers and wildlife reserves in which 60 different wild bird species have been seen including the tawny owl and sparrowhawk. An interesting, vibrant and very accessible small London park, though it can be overused on a hot summer day.

HORNIMAN MUSEUM GARDENS

See illustrations 2, between pages 32 and 33, and 23, between pages 96 and 97

Address: 100 London Road, Forest Hill, London SE23; **Tel**: 020 8699 1872; **Owner**: Horniman Public Museum & Public Parks Trust; **Location**: On South Circular Road, 5 mins walk from centre of Forest Hill; **Transport**: Forest Hill train station; Bus 176,185,312,P4,352; **Entrance**: Free; **Opening Times**: Daily 8am-dusk. Closed 25 Dec; **Other Information**: animal enclosure, bandstand, cafe, disabled access, dogs on leads only, events, parking in surrounding streets, toilets; **Seasonal Features**: May, June, July, August; herbaceous border, horse chestnuts, Indian bean tree, roses, summer bedding, sunken garden, wisteria

The gardens of the intriguing Horniman Museum cover 16 acres of hillside and are beautifully maintained, tranquil and well stocked with a wide range of plants. The main attractions are a rose garden with an outer rose and wisteria arbour and a sunken garden with a good display of summer bedding. There are also evergreen shrubberies, colourful herbaceous borders and a hillside rockery from which you can enjoy distant views of both town and country and admire the bandstand, possibly with band. The Dutch barn, opposite the bandstand, is an educational centre while the Victorian conservatory, built in 1894, is used for special events.

The majority of the Horniman Gardens is made up of sweeping lawns with some notable mature trees such as the corkscrew willow, Indian bean tree, swamp cypress and a number of oaks. At the top of the hill is a sunken flowerbed in which boldly hued bedding plants such as yellow and red celosia balance the lower beds. In the surrounding raised beds are palms, castor oil plants and a large cherry, Indian bean tree and gracious cedar look quietly on. Many benches here provide relaxing views or you may prefer to stroll around the large, hilltop herbaceous border containing sunflowers, acanthus and daisies and an analemmatic sundial where your shadow will tell the time.

A new extension to the Museum has recently been built with the main visitor entrance off the Chestnut Avenue. The areas round here and along the Museum's London Road frontage have been newly landscaped with an interesting variety of plants while the water garden provides a tranquil spot to rest and enjoy the views and fine displays of spring bulbs. The best time of year to see the gardens is probably June to August when the roses and herbaceous borders are flowering though the sunken garden looks good from spring to autumn and the garden has a spread of spring bulbs.

HYDE PARK *See illustration 5, between pages 32 and 33*

Address: Hyde Park, London W2; **Tel**: 020 7298 2100; **Owner**: The Royal Parks;
Location: Between Knightsbridge and Bayswater; **Transport**: Lancaster Gate & Marble Arch tubes (Central Line), Hyde Park Corner & Knightsbridge tubes (Piccadilly Line); Bus 2,8,9,10,12,14,16,19,22,36,73,74,82,94,137; **Entrance**: Free; **Opening Times**: Daily, dawn-midnight; **Other Information**: Bandstand, boating, children's playground, disabled access, dogs welcome on parkland, events, fishing, horse riding, restaurants, swimming, toilets; **Seasonal Features**: January, February, April, June, July, August, October, November, December; formal bedding, rose garden, witch hazels, coloured willows, autumnal trees

Hyde Park consists of 350 acres of open landscape just where it's most needed, right in the centre of London's throbbing heart. The land was owned by the Benedictine monks of St Peter, Westminster, until 1536 when it was given to Henry VIII who wanted it as a private hunting ground. For the next 100 years it was used as such until James I allowed restricted access and it became popular as a place in which to escape the smell and dirt of the expanding city. In the mid-18th century Queen Caroline, wife of George II, separated off the western-most 200 acres to form the grounds of Kensington Palace and created the Serpentine Lake. By the 19th century the park was a venue for national celebrations and Queen Victoria's Great Exhibition was held there in 1851.

Hyde Park has historically been a showpiece for bedding plant arrangements. The Victorians loved bold and elaborate displays with a touch of exotica and bananas and even cannabis would be added to their flowerbeds to give them a sub-tropical feel. The new rose garden by Hyde Park Corner Underground Station is worth a visit from June to August. It has a variety of soft-textured, pale flowers alternating with brighter, more formal beds. The whole is enclosed by pergolas with old fashioned roses and clematis. There is more summer bedding at Victoria Gate on the northern border of the park up by Lancaster Gate Underground Station.

Another summer feature is the meadow area south west of Marble Arch which you can reach via a stroll up the tree lined Broad Walk to the

notorious Speaker's Corner and Tyburn Memorial, where the public
gallows are reputed to have stood menacingly for 200 years. Grass in the
meadow is left to grow long, then cut and bailed at the end of July, thus
providing a traditional grassland ecosystem.

In autumn and winter it is pleasant to relax by the park's sheltered dell
garden located at the eastern end of the Serpentine Lake. It is Victorian in
style with seating and adjacent cafe. A stream escapes from the languid
Serpentine to run briskly through the little garden overhung by massive
London plane trees, a Caucasian elm and a strawberry tree. Moss, ferns,
hazels, waterlilies and gunnera all enjoy the humidity while exotica such
as corkscrew willows, a lovely magnolia and coloured acers stand further
back. For winter interest a paperbark maple with brightly coloured bark
can be found just across Rotten Row from the dell and a nearby Holocaust
memorial stands amongst a little grove of silver birch.

You can fish or boat on the Serpentine Lake, swim at its Lido, or simply
stroll or sit and watch others doing so. There is also an active program of
sport and children's activities in the park. For details contact the Park
Manager, tel: 020 7298 2100. With comprehensive sign-posting and a whole
host of footpaths there is plenty to see and plenty of space for everyone in
Hyde Park; but if it's plants you're after, you have to be prepared for a
walk.

KENSAL GREEN CEMETERY   *See illustration 19, between pages 96 and 97*

Address: Harrow Road, London W10; **Tel:** 020 8969 0152 **Owner**: General Cemetery
Company; **Transport**: Kensal Green tube (Bakerloo Line); Bus 18,52,302; **Entrance**:
Free; **Opening Times**: Daily, Apr-Sept 10am-6pm (Bank Hols 10am-1.30pm), Oct-
Mar 10am-5pm; **Other Information**: Guide dos only, guided tours every Sunday 2
pm from Anglican Chapel; **Seasonal Features**: March, April, May; wild flowers in nature
conservation area in oldest, central section, butterfly garden at main gateway

The Cemetery of All Souls at Kensal Green was established in 1832 and
has been operated ever since by the General Cemetery Company who have
created a large, landscaped park with avenues of mature trees leading to
grand, classical-style buildings. There are more free-standing mausoleums
here than in any other cemetery in the country and no fewer than three
catacombs. The colonnaded Anglican Chapel positioned near the centre
has beneath it a foreboding Victorian catacomb with a capacity of about
4,000 coffins. Back in the daylight, there is a large nature conservation area

in the older part of the cemetery where buttercups, coltsfoot and asters grow amongst the graves and the grass is left uncut until late summer.

An avenue of ornamental planes and horse chestnuts leads from the main entrance to the Anglican Chapel and hollies line the front of the building. Daffodils can be found along the main thorough-fares in spring when bluebells and primroses can also be spotted making the most of sunlight early in the year. Near the main entrance a butterfly garden developed by the London Wildlife Trust contains over thirty different types of blue and yellow flowered plants. These are in full bloom in midsummer when an array butterflies feed from them. At the other end of the cemetery lie the Crematorium and Gardens of Remembrance which have a sombre calm of their own.

Kensal Green Cemetery contains a good balance of shaded and open areas, in the former you will find mostly ivy, ferns, moss, lichen and the occasional patch of fungi. There are many famous names to watch out for on the imposing sarcophagi as well as towering temples and intriguing vaults and touching mementoes on the multitude of gravestones. As you wander the paths past quiet, limbless stone figures, and sunlight glistens through trees, a peace and restfulness fills the air.

KENSINGTON GARDENS   *See illustration 25, between pages 96 and 97*

Address: London W2; **Tel**: 020 7298 2100; **Owner**: The Royal Parks; **Location**: Between Bayswater Road & Kensington Road; **Transport**: Lancaster Gate & Queensway tubes (Central Line), High Street Kensington tube (District & Circle Lines); Bus 9,10,12,27,28,31,49,52,70,94, 148, 274; **Entrance**: Free; **Opening Times**: Daily, 6am-dusk; **Other Information**: Art gallery, disabled access, dogs welcome, events, restaurant, toilets; **Seasonal Features**: March, April, May, June, September, October; formal bedding, flower walk, sunken water garden, autumnal trees

It was Queen Caroline, wife of King George II, who in the mid 18th century divided off 200 acres of land from Hyde Park to form Kensington Gardens. The fashion then was for stately avenues of trees and vast expanses of water stretching to the horizon, and these were amply provided. Today many are still in evidence along with a whole host of impressive statues, memorials and some beautiful flower beds which have been added over time.

Kensington Palace dominates the western end of the gardens as it serenely surveys the streams of visitors flocking past every day. To the north of the Palace is a sunken garden, fit for royalty, but there for us all to see for free. It can only be viewed through openings cut in the pleached lime trees that encircle it but it is certainly a vision to behold. Tiers of densely planted, immaculately maintained flower beds step down to an inner rectangular pond with lovely waterlilies and antique lead cisterns. There is absolutely nothing to spoil the view and the colour scheme is subtly managed, being soft and pale at the top and brighter and bolder near the bottom where the colours are reflected back from the water. The whole effect is quite beautiful.

The other area of impressive planting is by the newly cleaned Albert Memorial, another of the garden's artistic marvels. This is the flower walk which is in contrast a relaxed setting, well screened from nearby traffic, with some interesting old weeping trees, palms, and succulents. The flower beds on either side of the sheltered path curve in and out and are well stocked and framed by luscious dark evergreens. They are at their best in spring and summer and the abundance of blossom, means it is often worthwhile resting on one of the benches to appreciate the colour and scents on offer. Half way along the flower walk a little path leads down into an area planted for spring with camellias, azaleas and rhododendrons.

Dividing up the garden's avenues of trees are the Round Pond and Long Water, with formal Italian gardens at one end containing the standard stone vases, statues and fountains. A recent additional feature is the Diana, Princess of Wales' Memorial Playground which, even though for children up to the age of 12, does offer some interesting seaside planting with ornamental grasses and bamboos wavering over herbaceous species. Adults without children can visit the playground from 9.30-10am each day

For those with an interest in modern art the Serpentine Art Gallery should not be missed. Dividing up the avenues of trees are the Round Pond and Long Water with the formal Italian gardens at one end containing standard stone vases, statues and fountains. Refreshments can be found in the beautiful 18th century orangery by Kensington Palace and time spent in Kensington Gardens can be both peaceful and rewarding, although you may find it overcrowded in peak season.

KENSINGTON ROOF GARDEN

Address: 99 Kensington High Street, Kensington, London W8 **Tel**: 020 7937 7994 **Owner**:Virgin Hotels Ltd; **Location**: On roof of GAP, entrance on Derry Street off Kensington High Street; **Transport**: High Street Kensington tube (District & Circle Lines); Bus 9,9A,10,27,28,31,49; **Entrance**: Free; **Opening times**: Subject to change

– visitors must telephone to check availability; **Other Information**: No dogs, restaurant and bar available to prebooked parties on Thurs and Sat only; **Seasonal Features**: June, July, August, October, November; roses, lavender, rosemary, vines, Virginia creeper

A real gem awaits one six floors up on top of the GAP Department Store far from the frantic pace and daily bustle of Kensington High Street. At 30 metres above the ground there is a tranquil one-and-a-half acre roof garden which, when it was planted in 1938, was the largest of its kind in Europe. It supports three distinct habitats – a Moorish-style Spanish garden with palm trees and canal, a lush English woodland garden and a formal Tudor garden. Flamingoes languish in the surreal setting and ducks seem at home in their high-rise ponds, criss-crossed by paths and bridges leading to peep-holes revealing magnificent panoramic views of the city.

The soil is no deeper than two metres and it is amazing that over 500 varieties of trees and shrubs survive up here. Wisteria garlands ancient stone pillars around an Elizabethan herb garden and autumnal vines and Virginia creeper writhe around ornate Spanish columns. Roses also thrive free from aphids which do not survive more than 15 metres above ground.

KENWOOD HOUSE GARDENS

Address: Hampstead Lane, London NW3; **Tel**: 020 7973 3893; **Owner**: English Heritage; **Location**: North end of Hampstead Heath; **Transport**: Highgate tube (Northern Line); Hampstead Heath train station; Bus 210; **Entrance**: Free; **Opening Times**: Daily Summer 7am-8.30pm, Winter 7am-dusk (approx. times only – tel for actual times); House Apr-Sept 10am-6pm (Oct 10am-5pm, Nov-Mar 10am-4pm); **Other Information**: Cafe, disabled access, dogs on leads only, parking, toilets; **Seasonal Features**: May, April, May, June, July, September, October; wild flowers, herbaceous borders, woodland, rhododendrons, autumnal trees

A broad, leafy avenue of mature horse chestnuts leads down to Kenwood House from Hampstead Lane. However when you reach the house you are greeted by an elegant, almost dainty, snow-white building that perches prominently on its terrace presiding over lawns sweeping down to lakes, and woods with wonderful views of the heath and city.

At the back and side of the house rhododendrons steal the show in their masses in May and their blossom is definitely worth seeing. From the terrace at the front you can rest to admire the panoramic view of the lawns and two large landscaped lakes – Wood Pond and Thousand Pound Pond.

These are surrounded by more mature trees and an avenue of limes marches diagonally down to the water's edge. The attractive sham bridge on the Thousand Pound Pond is an exact replica of the elegant 18th century construction, Including one upside-down baluster. On the western end of Kenwood House is a densely planted ivy arch and the ornate, embellished frontage of the house contrasts well with the dark green foliage of the ancient oaks, beeches and chestnuts dotted on the lawns.

Another feature of the gardens are the modern sculptures by artists such as Henry Moore and Barbara Hepworth which look impressive in so spacious a setting. There are also hay meadows on the western side of the house which change colour from May to July and if you walk past the cafe and up a small hill to the east of the building you will find a gazebo with another mesmeric view. This looks across the City towards Greenwich and you can pick out St Paul's Cathedral and Westminster on a clear day. Carry on along this route and you will find the old kitchen garden which is sheltered, peaceful and at its most colourful and fragrant from June to August. A high wall protects it from the road and heath and inside you can relax and admire summer borders, herbs and the ancient sundial stones. In August and September a large border of cosmos brightens up the western wall.

Finally, to the north of the house you can find remnants of ancient woodland dominated by oak and beech. Being old, broad-leaved woodland, it is species-rich and in April and May supports wood anemones, bluebells and foxgloves amongst much else on the woodland floor. Treecreeper, woodpeckers and nuthatch have all been seen here and English Heritage runs a series of lectures and guided walks throughout the year based on the 112 acre estate.

LADY VENICE'S GARDEN

Address: Regent's Canal, Little Venice, London W2; **Owner**: Mr Moore; **Location**: Regent's Canal, just above confluence with Grand Junction Canal; **Transport**:Warwick Avenue tube (Bakerloo Line); **Entrance**: Free; **Opening Times**: Daily; **Other Information**: Disabled access to street only, garden viewed from railings on Blomfield Road, nearby Rembrandt Gardens and Waterside Cafe; **Seasonal Features**: April, May, June, July, August, September, October; kaleidoscope of colour; container garden on colourful narrowboat with petunias, geraniums, lobelias, iberis, pansies, impatiens, alyssum, ivy, dahlias, etc.

It is a pleasure to explore the banks of Little Venice with its gently bobbing colourful narrow boats, its shady avenues of mature, London plane trees and its noble stuccoed villas set back across the dappled streets. As you wend your way around the maze of towpaths you can enjoy the houseboat garden plots, visit the Clifton Nurseries on Clifton Villas or stop for refreshments at the waterside cafe in a narrow boat moored by the Grand Junction. There is one garden here however that you should not miss for whatever the time of year it adds a touch of brilliance to the canal and is an exhibition of burgeoning colour.

The garden in question adorns a narrow boat known as 'Lady Venice' which is moored on Regent's Canal, just above the confluence with the Grand Union Canal. She is very obviously painted in bright blue and yellow and although the towpath immediately adjacent to her is private you can admire her garden from the overhanging railings and this alone is certainly worth the trip . On her roof rests a stylish black gondola accompanied by a group of white china swan planters with pink pelargoniums. Other pots, boxes, and troughs line the roof and towpath – many with traditional bargee's floral designs – and hanging containers are suspended from the boat and railings. A flower bed has been dug along the far side of the towpath and roses, ivies and wisteria grown up the railings which are shaded by the domineering London planes. The colour, which is present all year but is especially intense in summer, is provided by a glorious mixture of asters, cherry tomato, dahlias, fuchsias, geraniums, impatiens, lobelias, oleander, nasturtiums, pansies, and petunias. Yucca, fir, holly and much else besides provide textural interest and alyssum and herbs fill the air with a sweet fragrance as the canal gently ripples by.

LAMBETH COMMUNITY CARE
CENTRE GARDEN National Garden Scheme (NGS) see note on page 30

Address: Monkton Street, London SE11; **Owner**: Lambeth Primary Care Trust; **Location**: Monkton Street, off Kennington Road; **Transport**: Elephant & Castle tube (Northern & Bakerloo Lines); Bus 3,109,159,360; Opening Times: NGS annual open day only (see NGS book); **Other Information**: Disabled access, guide dogs only, plant sales, teas; **Seasonal Features**: Laburnums, spring blossom

Sitting atop the rubble of the old Lambeth hospital, this is a half acre garden which, thanks to a very enthusiastic, part-time gardener, completely defies its poor soil and brightens up many lives. Nestled away behind Lambeth

Lambeth Palace Garden

Community Care Centre it provides a therapeutic haven for the patients, their families, staff and visitors alike and time and again wins the cup for the best London hospital garden. An undulating lawn leads from the Care Centre patios to colourful beds containing numerous flowering perennials backed by Japanese maples and a spreading Indian bean tree. Interesting foliage is provided by bamboos, hellebores and hostas while a large cherry tree, mulberry and weeping pear display cheerful spring blossom. In early June a memorable *Fremontodendron californica* bathes a sidewall with it's yellow flowers and a mini laburnum avenue blazes from the back border.

As you follow the path and handrail through and over the garden you will discover a peaceful rose garden and secluded, hedged alcove with entrancing, elegant statue. There are plenty of enticing seats and comfortable viewing areas and even a small tropical conservatory with running water, stained glass windows and abundant plantlife. Colourful tubs adorn the patio area and overhead a clematis-clad bridge leads to an open terrace. The extensive plant sales and teas found here on the National Garden Scheme open day fund all the new planting and, if lucky, you may spot the feral cat lurking among the borders.

LAMBETH PALACE GARDEN   National Garden Scheme (NGS): see note on page 30

Address: Lambeth Palace Road, London SE1; **Owner**: Church Commissioners for England; **Transport**: Westminster tube (District & Circle Line), Lambeth North tube (Bakerloo Line), Waterloo tube (Bakerloo & Northern Lines); Waterloo train station; Bus 3,10,44,76,77,159,170,344; **Opening Times**: NGS annual open day (see NGS book), the annual North Lambeth Parish Fete (always last Sat. in June), group tours from Feb-Dec can be booked on tel. 020 7898 1191; **Other Information**: Disabled access, guide dogs only; **Seasonal Features**: March, April, June, July; daffodils, roses, spring bulbs, woodlands

Lambeth Palace garden is the oldest and second largest private garden in London. The monks of Rochester laid out the garden, which has been the London home of the Archbishops of Canterbury since the end of the 12th century. The garden was greatly restored by Lady Runcie, a former Archbishop's wife and development still continues to provide a garden that is a resource to the Ministry of the Archibishop and the many charities that he supports. If you venture inside the high boundary wall on one of the annual open days you will receive a friendly welcome and find a spacious, attractive and relaxing garden with a good balance of old and new. There are several commemorative trees and some beautiful statues commissioned from young artists. The Palace, towers and chapels which date from the 13th century give an air of utter permanence and stability and keep a watchful eye on proceedings.

The central main lawn and field dominate the garden and set off the buildings well. The two are separated by a large rose terrace dating back to the early 1900's well-stocked with pink, white and red varieties. Beside this lies a lavender hedge and two herbaceous borders which give good summer colour. A pleached lime screen under planted with dark blue agapanthus completes the soft colour scheme with which one can relax on the open lawn.

Around the pavilion mound are planted clusters of daffodils, other spring bulbs and some quite spectacular trees. At the far end as one sits to enjoy the view there is a pond replanted in 1995 with lilies and irises and a wild flower meadow with native trees which acts as a haven for butterflies and other wildlife. On each side of the main lawn woodland planting provides shelter for some shade-loving species as well as hellebores, snowdrops and fritillaries which grow all around the garden. A herb garden near the entrance gives the visitor a taste of what has for centuries been grown in the monastic garden at Lambeth Palace. As one glances across at the startling daffodils and magnificent trees or relaxes on one of the many seats dotted around, it is encouraging to know that a beautiful place with so much history attached can remain at peace in the heart of London today.

LINCOLN'S INN FIELDS

Address: Holborn, London WC2A; **Owner**: Lincoln's Inn; **Transport**: Holborn tube (Central & Piccadilly Lines); Bus 8,22B,25,501,521; **Entrance**: Free; **Opening Times**: Daily, dawn-dusk; **Other Information**: Guide dogs only, Sir John Soane's Museum on square – admission free; **Seasonal Features**: May, August; cherry blossom, roses, trumpet creeper

The Old Square at Lincoln's Inn Fields contains a remarkably unspoilt slice of history containing the four Inns of Court founded in the 14th century. The London plane trees are giants and complement the remarkable building of Lincoln's Inn Library which was once the Great Hall dating from 1845.

A sombre quiet pervades the square and you can take your time to stroll around the paths and enjoy the ancient mulberry trees, gnarled wisteria, still pond, flower borders and very ornate Brewster-designed iron gates, all beneath the leafy shade of the magnificent London planes. There are immaculate, untouched lawns, a well kept rose bed and a bright scarlet trumpet creeper (*Campsis radicans*). To reach the rest of the garden located in the main Square you must leave the secluded grandeur of the Old Square and cross the barrier at the Porter's Gate.

Here you find an interesting subtropical garden with bamboos, tree ferns, spiky succulents and soft pampas grasses. The majestic plane trees are again evident casting a welcome shade on hot summer days over tennis courts and a bandstand. There is some colourful annual bedding to be seen and in April and May spring blossom illuminates the shrub borders. As you wander round the Square's perimeter you will see some attractive surrounding buildings and the Sir John Soane's Museum is well worth a visit if you have the time.

LONDON WILDLIFE GARDEN CENTRE

Address: 28 Marsden Road, London SE15; **Tel:** 020 7252 9186; **Owner**: London Wildlife Trust; **Transport**: East Dulwich train station; Brixton tube (Victoria Line); Bus 37,176; **Entrance**: Free; **Opening Times**: Most days 10.30am-4.30pm, tel. for details; **Other Information**: Events, no dogs, plant sales, Tue-Thurs & Sun, 11am-4pm, (herbaceous plant & native tree nursery), visitor centre/classroom; **Seasonal Features**: May, June, July; wild flowers

In 1990 a patch of derelict land in Peckham, South East London, underwent a major transformation to win the Times/Royal Institute of British Architect's 'Green Building' award two years later and become the London Wildlife Trust's Garden Design Centre. Today a 0.6 acre site includes a wildlife garden with various habitats accommodating busy insects, amphibians and birds. A large plant sales area can be found as well as an environmental building with a green roof of stonecrops and house leeks. The mass of stonecrops on the roof flower in July producing a carpet of yellow.

To enter and leave the garden you pass through a pergola of scrambling passionflowers, roses, hops and vines. Next to the visitor centre is a series of reedbeds which collect water running off the building's roof and feed into a pond. Meadowsweet, waterlilies and rushes all flourish here and, as at other spots around the garden, a bench is provided for you to sit and watch for wildlife. In the centre of the garden saplings are grown for sale through the winter (trees are sold Nov-Mar, herbaceous plants are sold April-Oct). Only native tree species are sold and details can be obtained by telephoning 020 7252 9186.

In midsummer the garden reaches its peak with a mosaic of wild flowers in the summer meadow as well as the predominantly yellow and mauve blooms in the bumble bee border. Teasles produce statuesque lilac flowerheads here in August followed by spiky seedheads which attract finches. A well established climbing rose mingles with dark ivy foliage making a good habitat for nesting birds and a herb garden with its lavender, mint and thyme in full flower is attractive to both humans and insects. In spring wild plum, cherries and gorse bear their boughs of blossom and primroses unfurl in the shady fernery.

There is also a container garden and a kids' corner and the Centre runs in-house courses on planting and designing a wildlife garden and projects for adults with learning disabilities. If you want to visit a wildlife garden for information or just out of interest this is a good one to pick. You can see a number of established ecosystems in a peaceful setting as well as a working environmental building.

LONDON WILDLIFE TRUST NATURE RESERVES

The London Wildlife Trust works to protect wildlife throughout the Capital by conserving and enhancing natural habitats and ecosystems. They manage 57 nature reserves across Greater London and at some organise community events, run visitor centres and provide information packs. The following sites can all be reached on public transport but to find out about reserves in your area telephone the London Wildlife Trust on 020 7261 0447.

The Chase (Dagenham, Essex)
Entrance: on Dagenham & Upper Rainham Roads, Elm Park; **Tel**: 020 8593 8096; **Transport**: Dagenham East tube; Bus 174; **Open**: at all times;

Large nature reserve with wetlands, reedbeds, woodland and pasture attracting many animals and birds including woodpeckers and kingfisher. A large variety of wild flowers such as water crow-foots, spiny restharrow, clover and storksbill flourish in the 120 acre haven available to them.

Gunnersbury Triangle (London W4)
Entrance: on Bollo Lane, opposite Chiswick Park tube station; **Tel**: 020 8747 3881; **Transport**: Chiswick Park tube; Bus H40; **Open**: Tues-Sun in summer (April-Sept); Tues, Fri & Sun in winter (tel. for details);

A hidden woodland of birch and willow encompassing ponds and glades where wildlife can be glimpsed if you are quiet. Fungi and ferns are found in abundance, wild flowers grow near the clearings and the silver birches give a colourful autumnal display.

The Ripple (Barking, Essex)
Entrance: on Thames & Renwick Roads; **Tel**: 020 8591 0524; **Transport**: Barking tube; Bus 369; **Open**: at all times;

Hundreds of orchids now flower every May and June in what was once riverside industrial wasteland. Silver birches form a woodland which looks attractive in spring and autumn and a summer meadow is carpeted with wild flowers such as viper's bugloss.

Sydenham Hill Wood, Cox's Walk (London SE26)
Entrance: on Crescent Wood Road, off Sydenham Hill; **Tel**: 020 8699 5698; **Transport**: Sydenham Hill train station; Bus 3,63; **Open**: at all times;

This is a well established broadleaf woodland with a colourful variety of Victorian garden escapees, wild flowers, shrubs and trees lived in by some rare animals and birds. Bluebells, wood anemones and greater stitchwort all flower in spring along with masses of cherry blossom near to the meadow. Foxgloves and rosebay willowherbs give summer displays and there are autumn colours worth seeing along Cox's Walk which is an old avenue lined with oaks in which you may glimpse nuthatch and a green woodpecker.

Fishpond Wood & Beverley Meads (London SW20)
Entrance: Barham Road; **Transport**: Raynes Park train station; Bus 200; **Open**: all times;

In summer delicate blue forget-me-not flowers speckle the bank of the stream that wends through Fishpond Woods on Wimbledon Common. Mature oaks guard a patch of old, species-rich grassland which leads into hazel woodland. This bears a carpet of bluebells in May when wild flowers on the banks of the ponds are coming into bloom.

MARBLE HILL PARK

Address: Richmond Road, Twickenham, Middlesex TW1; **Tel**: 020 8892 5115; **Owner**: English Heritage; **Transport**: Richmond tube (District Line); St Margaret's train station; Bus 33,90,290,H22,R68,R70; **Entrance**: Free; **Opening Times**: Park open daily, 7.30am-dusk: House open 1 Apr-30 Sept, daily 10am-6pm; 1-31 Oct, daily 10am-5pm; 1 Nov-31 Mar, Wed to Sun 10am-4pm (closed 24-26 Dec, 1-18 Jan); **Other**

Information: Cafe, dogs welcome, events, picnics; **Seasonal Features**: May, June, July; limes, horse chestnuts, black walnut

Marble Hill House is a Palladian villa standing proudly amidst spreading lawns on the banks of the Thames in Richmond. Avenues of stately trees complement the house both encircling the park and lining various walks leading from the centre. The trees are mainly horse chestnut and lime which are attractive in spring and there is a notable specimen of a black walnut from the early 18th century which is one of the largest of its type in the country. In 1979 it stood at 92 ft. high.

In a shady area near the house hides a little ice house and a grotto stands by the east shrubbery from where, in winter, you get a particularly clear view of Richmond Hill across the river. Both features help transport you back in time to the 18th century when grottos were very fashionable and ice had to be kept packed in straw in a specially built ice house in the garden. Marble Hill House itself was built from 1724-29 for Henrietta Howard, mistress of George II, and the gardens were laid out in the 1740's.

The expansive lawns are now used mainly for sports pitches and for outdoor events in summer but the park also makes a good fresh walk and contains a cafeteria in the old stable block. Marble Hill Park forms a very open and relaxing green space in the heart of the congestion that is London. It is bordered on the other side of the river by Ham House and a frequent ferry service links the two.

MARIE CURIE CANCER CARE FIELDS OF HOPE

Marie Curie Cancer Care is a major charity which nurses cancer patients in their own homes. Its emblem is the daffodil, a universal symbol of hope, and in a special campaign the Charity plants thousands of these in large areas around the country in designated 'Fields of Hope'. Sited always in very visible, public places the fields of daffodils may contain anything from 2000 to 17000 bulbs and never fail to give an extremely vivid and dramatic display when they flower in March and April.

In London, Fields of Hope are planted in the following locations:

North
East End Rd, Finchley N3 (above North Circular Rd)
Hampstead Heath NW3 (south end of Heath)

81

South

Elephant & Castle SE1 (on the large, northernmost roundabout at the E. & C. junction)
Camberwell Green SE5 (alongside Camberwell Rd)
Salter Road, Rotherhithe, Southwark SE16 (on bank in front of Redriff School)
Thames Barrier, Woolwich SE18 (by Thames Barrier Visitor Centre, Unity Way SE18)
Poynders Road SW4(on the South Circular at the junct. of Poynders Rd & Clarence Av.)

East

Bethnal Green E2 (east side of Cambridge Heath Rd, north of junct. with Roman Rd.)
Mudchute Farm E14 (on East Ferry Rd)
London City Airport E16 (on City Airport Approach Rd)
Royal Albert Way E16 (on Royal Albert Way, off the A112)
Tower Hill EC3 (on south side of Tower Hill, adjacent to Tower Gardens)

West
Polish War Memorial (off A40)

MIDDLE TEMPLE GARDENS

Address: Temple Lane, London EC4; **Tel**: 020 7427 4800; **Owner**: Middle Temple; **Location**: The Temple (between Embankment and Strand); **Transport**: Temple tube (Circle & District Lines); Bus 4,11,15,23,26,76,171A; **Entrance**: Free; **Opening Times**: May, June, July, September, Mon-Fri, 12-3pm; **Other Information**: Disabled access, no dogs; **Seasonal Features**: June, July; wisteria, herbaceous border, roses

When you turn to wander up Temple Lane from the Embankment you enter a world of gardens and buildings that has changed little since the 12th century when the Knights Templar occupied the site and built a round church which still survives. The Knights Hospitallers leased part of the site to lawyers in 1312 but this later reverted to the crown. In 1609, James I granted ownership of the Temple to the Benches of the Inner & Middle Temples. You are about to encounter some of London's oldest gardens; it was the Middle Temple garden where the red and white blossoms were plucked at the start of the Wars of the Roses in the 15th century, and in the Inner Temple the garden was flourishing before the Third Crusade in the

12th century. It is intriguing to wander round the surrounding courts and temples and to sit and muse on the past in such an unchanged environment.

The Lower Temple Gardens which lead down to the river are not open to the public but one can peer through the railings at the immaculate lawns, spring blossom and rose beds. The gardens of the Middle Temple are usually open from 12-3pm on weekdays in May, June, July and September. Keeping watch over the garden on three sides are the mediaeval edifices into which efficient lawyers are seen quietly retreating as you ponder the peace and beauty of their surroundings.

A sorbus tree, cherry tree and a rowan grow on the beautifully maintained lawn and the surrounding walls and railings support well established climbing roses, Virginia creeper, wisteria, clematis and sweet pea. The garden is divided widthwise by a colourful and textural herbaceous borders containing canna lilies, stachys and some bold bedding.

Above the dividing border a small, secluded lawn makes an ideal place to sit and watch the river below or wonder at the sights around you. Below it is a larger area of grass where you can stroll to admire an old rose bed containing a sundial and look back up at this oasis of London history. The adjacent Elm Court is a very attractive courtyard, open at all times, with a large cherry tree, central fountain and interesting, well-maintained herbaceous border.

MILE END PARK

Address: Mile End Park, London E1; Tel: 020 7264 4660; **Owner**: Tower Hamlets Borough Council; **Location**: Alongside Grove and Burdett Roads; **Transport**: Mile End tube (Central, District, Hammersmith & City Lines); Bus 8,25,277,323,339,D6; **Entrance**: Free; **Opening Times**: Daily, dawn-dusk; **Other Information**: Adventure park, arts park, arts building, climbing wall, cycle path, dogs welcome, ecology park, electric go-karts, pubs, restaurant, sports part, toilets; **Seasonal Features**: April, May, June, July; lavenders, pondside garden, wildflowers

Stretching out between the dark, placid Regent's Canal and the busy, bustling Grove and Burdett Roads, Mile End Park provides much more than a long strip of green in London's East End. Designed in 2000 as a Millennium Commission Lottery Project, it joins up 'seven parks within a park' and contains an ecology area, 'artspark' and terraced garden, each of which contain ponds or lakes. The sporting facilities include a climbing wall, football pitches, running track and sports stadium while children's playgrounds can be found at either end. No fewer than five pubs with their own parking can be found in the park and the nearby Ragged School Museum is well worth visiting.

The main path meanders along the length of the park and encompasses all the planted areas. Mile End Road is spanned by a 'green bridge' that gives good views down a gently curing bank of lavender to the watery artspark as well as across a chain of lakes and out over East London to Canary Wharf. Many young trees are growing well and will soon help to blanket out traffic. Formal flowerbeds can be seen at each of the park's main entrances and there is a small rose garden by the main bus stop. The terraced garden has been prolifically planted with colourful, leafy borders that overlook a cascading pond screened with bulrushes. In spring, a flurry of wildflowers fills the banked meadow areas and wildlife is gradually spreading out from the ecology park.

The park's southern end is dominated by the Mile End sports stadium and athletics track but a walk along the Regent's Canal towpath leads you back along the sheltered western side and gives a relaxing break from the highroad bustle. Some old industrial warehouses still loom over parts of the dark waters and contrast well with the bright flowerbeds up on the raised main path.

MORDEN HALL PARK

Address: Morden Hall Road, Morden, London SM4; **Tel**: 020 8545 6850; **Owner**: The National Trust; **Transport**: Morden tube (Northern Line); Morden Road train Station; Bus 80,93,118,154,157,163,293,393,421; **Entrance**: Free; **Opening Times**: Daily, gate from car park to Park closes at 6pm; **Other Information**: Craft workshops, disabled access, dogs on leads only, environmental centre, events, garden centre, guided walks, National Trust shop, parking, tearoom, toilets; **Seasonal Features**: May, June, July; rose garden, limes, horse chestnuts, riverwalk, mill ponds, ancient hay meadows

What was once a large and thriving country estate lying beside the River Wandle amid vistas of English countryside is now conserved and managed by the National Trust. Morden Hall ark is an oasis amid the ceaseless roar of traffic and the seemingly endless plains of suburbia. Enter the park gates via the car park for Morden Hall Garden Centre on Morden Hall Road and you can soon forget about traffic as you choose between wandering beside the briskly flowing river or taking the lime and chestnut avenue path through the ancient hay meadows.

Morden Hall Park was created by the Hatfield family who made their money from snuff milling in the 18th century. It contains an attractive

Georgian house built in about 1750, which is now a bar and restaurant, with some attractive grounds including rose and lavender beds and a large lawn bordered by a moat. In 1941 Gilliat Hatfield died and left the estate to the National Trust. Part of the land was compulsory purchased for new housing and roads but 125 acres remains as rich wildlife habitat in the form of ancient meadowland, marshland and woodland.

The walled kitchen garden which once served Morden Hall is now a garden centre and car park and includes a National Trust shop and cafe. Beyond the garden walls you will discover over 100 acres of historic parkland with rose gardens, mill ponds and interesting buildings to enjoy. An impressive avenue of lime and chestnut trees was planted in 1870 and this, as well as the rippling River Wandle, helps to link the park together as it wends through meadowland sparkling with wild flowers such as ox-eye daisies, cowslips, celandines and birds foot trefoil. Some trees are remarkable for their age; the rambling yew by the 18th century Morden Cottage is more than 500 years old and a particularly aged magnolia leans on the handsome stable block. In mid summer you should not miss the rose garden. This contains a ginkgo tree and a stream curves around the edge with bamboos flanking it at one end.

There are two old snuff mills on the river which were the basis of the creation of the whole park. Today one of the snuff mills is an environmental study centre for children – tel: 020 8687 0881. There are also craft workshops housed in the old stables and boiler house and guided walks round the park are held all year. No less than 110 different bird species have been seen in Morden Park and a kingfisher is spotted regularly. Indeed, as you sit watching dragonflies whirr round the old mill pond overhung by giant hands of gunnera and gnarled corkscrew willows, life seems very pleasant.

MUSEUM OF GARDEN HISTORY GARDEN

Address: Lambeth Palace Road, London SE1; **Tel**: 020 7401 8865; **Owner**: The Tradescant Trust; **Location**: In the former church and garden of St Mary-at-Lambeth, next to Lambeth Palace; **Transport**: Lambeth North Tube (Bakerloo Line); Bus 3,77,344,507,C10; **Entrance**: Voluntary donation; **Opening Times**: Daily 10.30am-5pm; closed mid Dec to early Feb; **Other Information**: Art exhibitions, cafe, dogs on leads only, events, museum of garden history, shop; **Seasonal Features**: March, April, May, June, July; herbs, knot garden, topiary

This is a 17th century replica knot garden, designed by The Marchioness of Salisbury, and filled with historic plants and skilful topiary. It nestles in the grounds of the historic church of St Mary-at-Lambeth which now houses the Museum of Garden History and lays claim to one of the largest collections of historic gardening tools in the country. Amongst the flowers lie the finely ornamented tomb of the John Tradescants, father and son, gardeners to Charles I & II, who introduced many plants from the New World. A second tomb is that of the notorious Captain Bligh of the Bounty.

In the centre of the garden is a variegated holly (*Ilex* 'Golden King') clipped in a spiral with surrounding beds containing examples of plants retrieved by the Tradescants from their 17th century plant collecting expeditions to Europe and America. Colourful spring flowers such as tulips, fritillaries, daffodils, primroses and pinks are followed in summer by roses, gladioli, wallflowers and *Daphne mezereum*. Many neatly trimmed herbs give a long seasonal interest and all are well labelled and maintained. Visitors can sit peacefully to admire the old walls clad in flowering climbers, ivy or Virginia creeper, listen to the babbling fountain or admire the tombs looming from their bed of rosemary and Solomon's seal. The garden is an oasis of colour, calm and wonderful aromas as the world passes by.

MUSEUM OF LONDON'S NURSERY GARDEN

Address: Museum of London, London Wall, London EC2Y; **Tel**: 020 7600 3699; **Owner**: Museum of London; **Location**: Museum of London; **Transport**: St Paul's tube (Central Line), Barbican tube (Circle, Hamm. & City, Met. Lines); Bus 8,11,15,23,25; **Entrance**: Free; **Opening Times**: Garden open 30th Mar-Oct; Mon-Sat 10am-5.20 pm, Sun 12-5.20 pm; **Other Information**: Disabled access, guide dogs only, events, museum exhibitions, parking, restaurant, shop, toilets; **Seasonal Features**: June, July; rose arbour

The history of London's plant nurseries from the Middle Ages to the 20th century is brought to life in a compact exhibition which wends around an internal courtyard in the Museum of London. Plants from, and information about, leading nurseries are displayed round the garden and jasmine and ivy trail down to a fernery in a shady space below. A sizeable ivy-clad alder tree stands at the centre and a tumbling stream flows rapidly round it over a narrow bed of slates. At either side are a large medlar and a small strawberry tree, both bearing bountiful fruit in autumn. As you wander round it is interesting to think how we have arrived at the variety of horticultural plants available to us today.

The first known London nurseryman was William the Gardener who supplied plants to Edward I in 1274-7 for new gardens at Westminster and the Tower of London. Red and white roses, willows and peach trees are shown here as examples of what he sold. In the 16th century the main nurseryman was Henry Russell of Westminster. His evergreens – sweet bay, cypress, yew and juniper – were only 2d each and roses were 4d a hundred. The greatest of London's early nurseries, from 1681–1851, was Brompton Park Nursery which provided trees to many large country estates. Those you see here are box, yew, citrus and clematis.

You can also witness an amusing display of clipped evergreens representing Cutbush's Nursery which traded from 1716–1922 and catered for a passing topiary craze. A rose arbour is based on a design from the early 20th century by John P. White and planted with a selection of Lee & Kennedy roses which flower in June and July. From the mid 18th century Loddiges' Nursery of Hackney set high standards of naming plants and held an extremely diverse collection. Scilla and anenome species are included in the beds here and as you continue on your way you can see how the exotic and ornamental plant species are creeping in.

The museum is packed with quality exhibits and outside the entrance is a good restaurant and a courtyard garden with trees, climbers, a lawn and raised beds to look down into while you drink your tea.

MYDDELTON HOUSE GARDENS

Address: Myddelton House, Bulls Cross, Enfield, Middlesex EN2; **Tel**: 01992 702200; **Owner**: Lee Valley Regional Park Authority; **Transport**: Turkey Street train station; **Entrance**: Entrance charge; **Opening Times**: Mon-Fri 10.00am–4.30pm (April-Sept) 10.00am–3.00pm (Oct-March) (except 25 Dec-1 Jan); Sundays (Easter-Oct), Bank Hols & National Gardens Scheme open days (see NGS book* for dates) 12-4 pm; **Other Information**: Guide dogs only, guided tours available if booked on tel. 01992 709849, parking, plant sales, refreshments, toilets; **Seasonal Features**: January, February, March, April, May, June, July, September, October, November; snowdrops, hostas, hellebores, crocuses, daffodils, euphorbias, bearded irises, wisteria, tulips, lilies, herbaceous borders, roses, summer bedding, cyclamens, autumn crocuses, autumnal trees, fruits & berries

Myddelton House Gardens were the inspiration of E. A. Bowles (1865–1954), a famous botanical artist and writer and an enthusiastic plant collector, who lived in the main house and was a generous local benefactor. As you wander down the twisting drive from the little entrance lodge with its own pretty front garden you are welcomed by a characterful, tranquil and much loved garden. There is a conservatory, a rock garden and a beautiful carp lake where huge fish occasionally leap from the water in an attempt to scratch their backs while sepulchral herons gather hopefully on the bank. From January through to early summer an alpine meadow and rock garden come alive with millions of snowdrops, crocuses and daffodils, etc.; later there are abundant tulips, roses, irises, wisteria and some showy lilies and in autumn many autumn crocuses, nerine lilies and cyclamens raise their delicate heads. This is designed very much as a year-round garden and even in deep winter at least three types of christmas rose (*Hellebore spp*) and many evergreens add colours which complement the mellow golden brick of the Regency house they surround. One constant attraction is a bed of golden, white and silver variegated and coloured leaved plants known as Tom Tiddler's Ground which was inspired by the fictional character who found a pot of gold at the rainbow's end.

Bowles had many plants named after him and he was vice president of the RHS for a number of years. He loved his garden, stocking it with rare and unusual plants and spending much time there, both writing and painting. After his death the house and grounds were acquired by the University of London's School of Pharmacy who used the kitchen garden to grow medicinal plants while the rest became overgrown with ivy and ground elder. In 1968 Lee Valley Regional Park Authority bought the house and gardens and in 1984 started to restore the latter to the style of Bowles.

This must be the only garden to contain a 'lunatic asylum' for plants and this is exactly what Bowles himself called it in 1909 as he gathered together in one bed all the plants which grew irrational in some way. The first lunatic was the corkscrew hazel. Later a twisted hawthorn, the hedgehog holly, green rose and a collection of cut-leaved elders were all added. Today many of the originals have been lost due to shading but cuttings remain and a hedgehog holly dated circa early 17th century is quite a phenomenon.

The National Collection of bearded irises is held in the gardens and consists of over 300 different iris species which flower in May. In April the tulip terrace is a broad belt of colour and from June the rose garden, which has been replanted with many of Bowles' original species, and includes tree peonies and camellias comes into bloom. The rose garden is dominated by the old Enfield Town Market Cross which was salvaged by Bowles from a local builder's yard. The original owner was fond of historical artifacts and near the entrance a petrified tree can be found standing amongst a group of old stones given by local school children. While exploring, you should peep into the Victorian conservatory tacked onto the end of Myddelton House as with its colourful, tiled floor, draping bananas, climbing roses, peculiar sago palm, giant cacti, brugmansia and magnificent Banksian rose, it feels both somewhat alien and melodramatic. Two life-size lead statues of ostriches stand comically amongst the vegetation and the bulbous cape lilies by the door can grow to almost two metres tall.

As you can gather there is much to see the whole year round at this incredibly interesting and beautiful garden. It was much cherished in its day by a real plantsman whose unique character reveals itself in the varied design of the garden and in some of the rare and unusual plants still remaining there today. Bowles himself wrote in his Trilogy, 'My Garden in Autumn and Winter', '*A touch of gold or crimson on the heady dark green foliage of late summer gives promise of the new picture that will grow clearer as the old one fades ...*'

* The National Gardens Scheme book, 'Gardens of England and Wales open for Charity', is published annually by the NGS and can be found in any large bookshop.

NATURAL HISTORY MUSEUM WILDLIFE GARDEN

Address:The Natural History Museum, Cromwell Road, London SW7; **Tel**: 020 7942 5725; **Owner**: Natural History Museum; **Transport**: South Kensington tube (District & Circle, Piccadilly Lines); Bus 14,74,C1; **Entrance**: Free; **Opening Times**: June to Aug, Tues,Thurs, Sun 1-4pm: guided tours May to Sept, daily at 12am & 3pm – tel. for details; **Other Information**: Disabled access, guide dogs only, café, shop & toilets in museum; **Seasonal Features**: April, May, June, July; pondside garden, wildflowers

In 1995 the Natural History Museum opened a well-researched wildlife garden in the grounds of their imposing Victorian edifice in the heart of west London. Ever since, it has blossomed and burgeoned and more than 600 species of plants and animals have been recorded there. In 1997 a detailed survey of its fauna and flora was carried out and will be repeated at 10-year intervals.

The garden features 8 different British lowland habitats. It's pond attracts frogs, newts and a visiting heron while sheep graze the meadow. Turf for the fertile chalk downland was imported from a disused quarry and peat for the fen was obtained by dredging ditches. At varying times of year the oak woodland brims with bluebells, anemones, ferns and fungi and the hedgerows with the blossom of hawthorn, field maple, crab apple and red campion. The heathland area welcomes spring with a splash of gorse, broom and, later, heather while dragonflies and damselflies bring the reedbed to life in early summer.

As you search out the wildlife, you can view the distinctive soil profiles found beneath the different habitats as well as slabs of limestone containing a 140 million year old dinosaur footprint. The garden, in the heart of the Capital, functions both as an educational resource and a valuable research subject. It is the museum's first living exhibition and is remarkable for the potential for wildlife conservation in the inner city that it displays.

17A NAVARINO ROAD GARDEN National Garden Scheme (NGS): see p30

Address: 17A Navarino Road, Hackney, London E8; **Tel**: 020 7254 5622; **Owner**: John Tordoff Esq.; **Transport**: Bethnal Green tube (Central Line); Hackney Central train station; Bus 242,30,38,277; **Opening Times**: NGS annual open day (see NGS book), private visits welcome for groups of 10 or more; **Seasonal Features**: Japanese garden, topiary, roses, azaleas

This small, private garden hidden away in east London is an education in space management with two distinct areas combining a classic formality with a calming informality; it must bring hours of pleasure to its owner. Certainly as a visitor you are impressed by the skill and imagination that goes into designing and maintaining a garden so full of delicate topiary, clear streams and ponds and a beautiful Japanese garden surrounded by ornamental species such as acers, bamboos and azaleas.

In 1996 the garden won the BBC Gardeners' World Competition for the most beautiful small garden in Britain. The first section is a formal Italianate style area with a central pond planted with cyperus and arum lilies and containing a fountain decorated with white doves. An encircling, clipped yew hedge and beds of variegated-leaved shrubs as well as potted herbaceous plants and rambling roses, wisteria and autumnal vines all crowd neatly around the rectangular pond and provide a long seasonal interest. Two peacocks have been immaculately cut from a lonicera species and stand by a ceanothus which is a delicate blue in summer. Roses abound in mid summer both on the house wall and in the garden and you must pass through a richly fragrant rose pergola to enter the Japanese garden.

This part of the garden is a Japanese landscape in miniature with forests, mountains, standing stones and valleys all covered in a dense layer of small-leaved mind-your-own-business (*Soleirolia soleirolii*). In the top corner stands a large Japanese temple and down across the plains trickles a stream which emerges from the base of a trail of variegated ivy, flowing over clipped box steps and into a clear, miniature lake at the bottom. An ornamental bridge means you can wander on paths round the Japanese landscape taking in its dwarf conifers and colourful surrounding bed. Otherwise you can sit by the little lake to enjoy the view and the continual running of the stream, as the head of a sleeping Buddha lies partly hidden in the bottom corner and a wisteria arbour rises high over the top.

NUMBER 1 POULTRY ROOF GARDEN *See illustration 14, between p96 and 97*

Address: Number 1 Poultry, London EC2R; **Owner:** Coq d'Argent; **Transport:** Bank/Monument tube (Northern, Central, District, Circle Lines); Bus 8,22B,26,501; **Entrance:** Free; Opening Times: Bar & Terrace, Mon-Fri 11.30am-10.30pm; Sat 6.30pm-10.30pm; Sun 12am-3pm; **Other Information:** Restaurant reservations 020 7395 5000, no dogs; **Seasonal Features:** January, February, April, May, August, September, November, December; roof garden, oak pergola with white wisteria & 'Uva Fragola' grapes, fruit trees, magnolia, herbs, roses, lawn with rows of clipped box leading to apex

As you soar swiftly up through the modern edifice that is Number 1, Poultry and leave behind a busy, polluted shopping centre and street at ground level your expectation of what is at the top also quickly rises. You will not be disappointed. The roof of the building is occupied by a glamorous restaurant, the Coq d'Argent, which owns probably the most remarkable roof garden in London from which you get a good view out across the City's many landmark buildings.

The garden itself was designed in 1985 by Arabella Lennox-Boyd although it was actually planted only in 1998. It is half an acre in size with a soil depth of 750 mm and includes sixteen mature trees including spring-flowering cherries, crab apples, magnolias and a hawthorn. Even in winter, roof gardens are always up to five degrees celsius warmer than normal gardens due to the heat generated by the building below. This renders many species unsuitable for the site.

The garden is divided into three main areas. The main dining and reception area is surrounded by a massive English oak pergola cloaked in white wisteria and sweet 'Uva Fragola' grapes which can be picked and eaten. Diners and visitors can see spring blossom, irises and camellias; summer flowering herbs, jasmine, buddleia and acanthus; autumnal fruit and berries and a mixture of year-round evergreen foliage. In contrast to the well-structured dining area there is an apex garden which is relatively soft and simple with uninhibited City views. The ground slopes gently down across wide grass areas in the centre to lines of box hedging which lead to the apex. The apex itself is punctuated by bold, stone spheres surrounded by a low wall – not for those with vertigo. The third and last part of the garden is the outer garden which features beech columns in planted *arms*, white roses and cotoneasters.

As a botanical setting for both a bar and a restaurant, or simply as a somewhere to sit back and enjoy the most superb views of London, the garden is stylish and interesting and both it and the bar and restaurant, of the Coq d'Argent are well worth a visit.

NUNHEAD CEMETERY

Address: Linden Grove, London SE15; **Tel:** 020 7732 9535 – Park Rangers; **Owner**: Southwark Council; **Transport**: Nunhead train station; Bus 484,343,P12; **Entrance**: Free; **Opening Times**: Daily Winter 8am-4pm, Summer 8am-7pm; **Other Information**: Dogs welcome, guided tour on last Sunday each month at 2.15 pm – free; **Seasonal Features**: March, April, May; wild flowers

You may find this cemetery both sad and beautiful, disturbing and restful. It is certainly a very atmospheric and memorable square mile inner city woodland and as you wander round the ruined Gothic chapel, looming mausoleums and 100 ivy-clad angels you may well become increasingly fond of the wildness and its tranquillity. Numerous gravestones of the long departed fall away from the main paths down into the dank undergrowth and off into the forest. Statues in varying states of dilapidation adorn larger tombs and many gravestones lean thankfully against their neighbours or one of the many nearby trees.

The cemetery was set up by the Victorians and is unusual in being located within woodland. Unfortunately most trees have not been thinned out and are now spindly and relatively unstable. They are mostly broadleaf species and form a dense canopy in summer with an undergrowth of ivy, moss, fungi and ferns amongst the graves and damp, rotting wood. In the centre and along the Brockley footpath on the eastern side, large areas have been cleared of trees and the light allows a scattering of wild flowers throughout the spring and summer.

A pond and picnic area are included in the cemetery and amongst its notable monuments are five War Graves, a Scouts' War Memorial, a Scottish Political Martyrs' Memorial, a catacomb and a ruined Anglican Chapel. An avenue of mature lime trees lined with massive family vaults leads to the chapel while rows of mature beeches flank another main forest route.

A £1.3m Heritage Lottery funded project completed in 2002 has enable restoration of the chapel, main entrances and 50 priority monuments. Nevertheless as you amble round this historic and forlorn place the smell of damp wood pervades the calm as woodland encroaches and gradually more tombstones tumble into the green hands of nature.

OSTERLEY PARK

See illustration 3, between pages 32 and 33

Address: Jersey Road, Isleworth, Middlesex TW7; **Tel**: 020 8568 7714; **Owner**: The National Trust; **Transport**: Osterley tube (Piccadilly Line); Syon Lane train station; Bus H91; **Entrance**: Free; **Opening Times**: Park open daily 9am-7.30pm (dusk if earlier); House open 1 Apr-31 Oct, daily, except Mon & Tues (closed Good Fri, open Bank Hols), 1-4.30pm; **Other Information**: Cafe, disabled access, dogs on leads only, events, parking, shop, toilets; **Seasonal Features**: January, February, March, April, May, September, October, November, December; bluebells, daffodils, cherry blossom, horse chestnuts, autumnal trees, cedars

Easily reached by car or via the Piccadilly line, Osterley Park is an estate of 650 acres and was for 300 years the largest park near London. Osterley House stands proudly at its heart, built by Sir Thomas Gresham, Chancellor of the Exchequer to Queen Elizabeth I, in about 1577. Robert Adam, a neo-classical architect, was commissioned by Robert Child to redesign the house in 1763 and it was he who produced the confident four-turreted exterior that both confronts and welcomes us today.

The park was originally laid out in formal Tudor style with walled gardens by the house. Sir William Chambers redesigned it in the 19th century creating more natural vistas with expansive lawns and lakes. In 1949 the 9th Earl of Jersey gave the house and park to the National Trust which has plans to restore the park to redisplay some of the Tudor style gardens for visitors. They have also started grazing the Great Meadow to the south west of the house with a herd of French Limousin cattle which add interest and improve the grassland as a habitat for insect and bird life. The RSPB conduct magical dawn walks at certain times of year to glimpse some of the birds in a large and unspoilt rural area.

The main drive to Osterley Park is an avenue of mature trees with daffodils giving splashes of seasonal colour. This serves as a gentle introduction to the impressive collection of trees you encounter at Osterley. Its magnificent cedars of Lebanon, which can be found on the lawn named after them, are almost 240 years old. All the ancient Osterley cedars somehow managed to withstand the destructive storms of 1987 and 1990 which swept south east Britain. On the same lawn stands an age-old cork oak tree – the bark of this species is used to produce corks for the drinks industry and the trees are grown in plantations on the continent. Elsewhere in the spacious, informal grounds you can amble round the Great Meadow, wondering at the history contained in clumps of 18th century oaks, hornbeams and horse and sweet chestnuts. Autumn is a special time with fiery reds and yellows of some unusual trees dotted in the wood bordering the lush meadow. Many evergreens around the meadow mean it is also attractive to visit through the winter. To conclude a visit to Osterley the visitor can relax among the flower beds in the former pleasure grounds by the Temple of Pan and stable block or wander further around the two lakes. There are many old magnolias, camellias and rhododendrons to be enjoyed in spring and although both Heathrow airport and the M4 are in earshot a surprising amount of wildlife seems to be at home here.

PECKHAM RYE PARK

Address: Peckham Rye Park, London, SE22; Tel: 020 8693 3791; **Owner**: Southwark Borough Council; **Transport**: Nunhead or East Dulwich train stations; Bus 12,37,63,78,312,484,P3,P12,P13; **Entrance**: Free; **Opening Times**: Daily, summer 8am-9pm, winter 8am-4.30pm; **Other Information**:Arboretum, café, car park, disabled access, dogs welcome, tennis courts, toilets, tree trail, trim trail; **Seasonal Features**: May, June; Japanese garden, roses, wildflowers

Peckham Rye Common, which lies beside the park, is one of the oldest recreation grounds, mentioned in the 14th century as an area for stag hunting. In the 19th century a notorious highwayman, 'Brockley Jack', plied his trade on the Common and it has since been used by locals for grazing animals and by the authorities for a prisoner of war camp.

Peckham Rye Park was opened in May 1894 and now contains a sizeable collection of mature trees with good autumnal displays of maples and oaks as well as attractive spring blossom. In June, the Sexby garden, located at the centre, is a pleasant place to sit and admire the roses, lavender and wisteria while the Japanese garden and two woodland areas are most colourful in April and May. A somewhat neglected lake lies beside the café, watched over by weeping willows, yews and a Bhutan pine. Other, more unusual trees are the corkscrew hazel, purple leafed hazel and a large hybrid ash that is half weeping, half straight.

The park is being redeveloped and, with Southwark Council's relatively good reputation for managing parks and gardens, it will be interesting to see what happens.

POSTMAN'S PARK

Address: King Edward Street, London EC1; **Tel**: 020 8477 3584; **Owner**: Corporation of London; **Transport**: St Paul's tube (Central Line); Bus 8,25,56,242; **Entrance**: Free; **Opening Times**: Daily, dawn-dusk; **Other Information**: Commemorative wall, disabled access, dogs welcome; **Seasonal Features**: May, June; formal bedding, herbaceous borders

Postman's Park was opened in 1880 and today stands as a refreshing, attractive and peaceful haven amidst the bustle and noise of surrounding modern city life. Taking its name from its proximity to the main postal sorting office on King Edward Street, the park is made up of land from three disused burial grounds: St Leonards, Foster Land; St Botolphs, Aldersgate and Christchurch, Newgate Street. Many gravestones and a lonely tomb linger in the park today and the church of St Botolph-without-Aldersgate and stands silently in one corner. A Christian open air meeting is held in the park each Monday at 1.15 pm from May to September.

In 1887 the painter, George Frederic Watts, conceived the idea of a national memorial to commemorate men and women who lost their lives saving others. He designed a shelter to this cause which was placed in Postman's Park and dedicated in 1900. It bears 50 plaques commemorating such people as Walter Peart and Harry Dean, driver and fireman of the Windsor Express who died saving their train and its passengers on 18 July 1898. This park has a calming and tranquil atmosphere which is enhanced by large trees looming overhead, undulating, verdant lawns and a lush herbaceous border effectively helping to seal off visitors and their thoughts from the outside world.

Many benches are provided and splashes of colour radiate from a well-maintained central flowerbed near the commemorative shelter. There is also a small rose bed near here and a semi-tropical bed with a large tree-fern. In front of the church is a round pond in which a fountain splashes unobtrusively whilst water plants such as irises and lilies stand sentinel-like round the edge and goldfish dart swiftly through the clear waters.

Fifty yards further down King Edward Street from Postman's Park in the direction of St Paul's Cathedral is a rose garden planted within some impressive ruins. This is worth visiting in late May and early-mid June when the roses are in full bloom. It consists of two large beds surrounded by box hedges and two wooden pergolas. You can sit in the garden and have a good view of St Paul's Cathedral although traffic noise is disturbing.

QUEEN'S PARK

Address: Harvist Road, Kilburn, London NW6; **Tel**: 020 8969 5661; **Owner**: Corporation of London; **Transport**: Queen's Park tube (Bakerloo Line); Bus 206; **Entrance**: Free; **Opening Times**: Daily, 7.30am-dusk; **Other Information**: Cafe, children's playground, disabled access, dogs welcome everywhere but ornamental garden, pets corner, sports facilities, toilets; **Seasonal Features**: June, July, August; ornamental garden with formal bedding

The thirty acres of Queen's Park in one of the most densely populated parts of London provides a welcome oasis of green with many mature trees, a relaxing ornamental garden and sports facilities ranging from boules to six all-weather tennis courts. Well maintained and managed in parts, such as the pets corner and the annual flower beds, which are changed frequently to reflect the seasons, it is left to nature to take its own course in other areas with some tree trunks lying on the ground to provide homes for wildlife.

A large, central, grassy space is surrounded by a band of mixed mature trees and in the northern end is a cafe with its own garden, children's corner and paddling pool. Sports facilities are dotted around and a bandstand nestles in the shade but for those looking for peace, pattern and botanical colour the garden in the south eastern corner is the place to be. This is meticulously kept with fine lawns and neat crescent and circular beds. Visitors are asked to keep to the paths and a series of benches are provided. A shield bed is raised at an angle to the path and skilfully planted up each year – can you recognize the design? Elsewhere in the garden conical, clipped yews, a tree of heaven and an old hawthorn add height and structure while fuchsias, ricinus, begonias, pelargoniums, canna lilies and nicotianas add a mixture of texture, shape and colour to the beds. A shrub border round the edge contains a mixture of philadelphus, cherries and roses. It has botanical interest from May through to September and is a very attractive place to while away some time below the grand London plane trees.

14. The well-established roof garden of Number 1, Poultry, in which visitors can relax far above the hectic city life below

15. A handsome classic temple in Gunnersbury Park presides over spring flowers

17. Queen Mary's Gardens, Regent's Park, with its swathes of summer rose colour and scent

16. *main picture:* The magnificent wisteria pergola in Fulham Palace Gardens overhangs a 19th-century knot garden

18. Every spring a carpet of crocuses transforms the Victoria Gate entrance of the Royal Botanic Gardens, Kew

19. *above:* Autumnal foliage aglow with the afternoon sun in Kensal Green Cemetery

20. *left:* A glimpse of autumn

22. *opposite top:* Autumn colours enhance the Japanese Gateway at the Royal Botanic Gardens, Kew

21. *opposite:* Seasonal shades highlight many autumn walks such as this in the Royal Botanic Gardens, Kew

23. A garden with colour, intrigue and a view at the Horniman Museum

24. The immaculate and colourful sunken garden at Hampton Court Palace

25. The marvellous sunken garden in Kensington Gardens – a horticultural phenomenon

26. The geometrical knot garden at Ham House punctuated by cones of box

27. A bold cedar tree amidst the glorious rose garden of Greenwich Park

28. An eccentric oak tree abides in Waterlow Park

RAVENSCOURT PARK

Address: King Street, Hammersmith, London W6; **Tel**: 020 8748 3020; **Owner**: Hammersmith & Fulham Borough Council; **Transport**: Ravenscourt Park tube (District Line); Bus 27,94,237,267,391,H91; **Entrance**: Free; **Opening Times**: Daily, 7.30am-dusk; **Other Information**: Bowling green, cafe, children's playground, conservation area, crazy golf, dogs welcome everywhere but scented garden, garden centre, netball, picnic area, sandpit/paddling pool, skateboard ramp, tennis courts, toilets, under-5s area; **Seasonal Features**: April, May, June, July; cherry blossom, scented garden, rose pergola

Ravenscourt Park is a well used community park providing facilities for many interests, ages and abilities in its relatively small space. There is a garden centre nestling under the railway arches at the southern end, a lake and a walled garden specially designed for the visually handicapped with scented plants in raised beds. An avenue of elderly cherry trees runs down the middle of the park and in April and May each year this becomes a glacier of blossom. Various large-leaved oaks, rowans, dwarf conifers and an old holly serve to bring year round colour to the main entrance area by King Street.

The main grassy sweep of the park is edged by a tree lined avenue to the east of which are various sports facilities. A group of towering, mature London plane trees dominates the main park and a sweet gum, sweet chestnut, catalpa and old mulberry all give autumnal interest. In the north of the park, an old cedar of Lebanon mushrooms over a skateboarding ramp which is located next to a small nature conservation area. Trees, shrubs and wild flowers have been planted there to encourage wildlife and the area is managed by Groundwork West London.

A secluded and colourful place to sit in Ravenscourt Park is the scented garden sited in a walled garden in the north west corner. This contains a central, round rose arbour and three corner rose beds. A large magnolia grows against one of the corners and one of the sides has a pleasant view into the park. Wisteria, ivy, jasmine and passionflower climb surrounding walls and mixed perennials such as rosemary and stachys pack the side borders. In the middle are raised, geometrical beds, particularly fragrant and colourful from June to August, and by the ornate entrance gate a large lavender bush throws out its scent to entice you in.

Around the lake you will find cedars, weeping willows, rhododendrons, maples and feathery pampas grass where the flocks of wildfowl have a very overgrown island to hide away on. A cafe is positioned by the lakeside and you can have a drink here before, perhaps, visiting the garden centre.

REGENT'S PARK   *See illustration 17, between pages 96 and 97*

Address: Marylebone, London NW1; **Tel**: 020 7486 7905; **Owner**: The Royal Parks; **Location**: Between Marylebone Rd & Prince Albert Rd; **Transport**: Regent's Park tube (Bakerloo Line), Great Portland Street & Baker Street tubes (Circle, Metropolitan & Hamm. & City Lines), St John's Wood tube (Jubilee Line) & Camden Town tube (Northern Line); Marylebone train station; Bus 2,13,18,27,30,74,82,113,135,139,159, 189,274,C2; **Entrance**: Free; **Opening Times**: Daily, 7am-dusk; **Other Information**: Bandstand, boating lake, cafe, children's playground, dogs welcome in park only, events, London Zoo, open air theatre, parking, sports facilities, toilets; **Seasonal Features**: April, May, June, July, August, September, October; spring blossom, herbaceous borders, formal bedding, begonia garden, rose garden, secret garden, autumnal trees

Regent's Park was once but a small part of the great Middlesex Forest. On the dissolution of the monasteries in the mid 17th century Henry VIII acquired the Manor of Tyburn and felled over 16,000 trees from the area to raise money to pay for his cavalry troops. This clearing was to become Regent's Park, kept mainly as a private Royal hunting ground until the 1840's when it was opened to the public to be used as recreation for the expanding city.

The park today has evolved largely from the plans of John Nash (1752-1835), Crown Architect and friend of the Prince Regent, who designed an ambitious private residential development set in parkland. It was to include some Classic villas each with their own grounds, one of which was to be the Prince Regent's own retreat – hence the park's name. The Regent's villa was in fact never built, but other villas were and stand majestically around the park. As one explores the rolling parkland and secluded gardens a number of large buildings, terraces, lakes and secret gardens reveal themselves.

Within the Inner Circle is a maze of herbaceous beds, Mediterranean style borders and a large rose garden collectively known as Queen Mary's gardens. ,The Royal Botanic Society created their gardens here in 1840, thereby originating a tradition of horticultural display in the park. The rose garden is peaceful and well-stocked with more than 60,000 roses of 400 different varieties. There is also a lake, cascades, a cafe and an open-air theatre. A sunken garden is used for seasonal bedding and begonias give a very vivid splash of colour in summer months.

If you investigate the northern boundary of the Inner Circle opposite the entrance to Queen Mary's rose garden you will find the opening to a 'secret garden', officially known as St John's Lodge garden. A wisteria walk leads you down to a circular rose garden from where sunken beds lead up to railings bordering the villa's forecourt. The secret garden is secluded and peaceful and contains a little arbour garden, scented plants, climbers, pleached lime circles and attractive sculptures which are all definitely worth exploring.

Leading south off the Chester Road, just five minutes' walk from the rose garden, are the formal Italianate Avenue gardens which are bold, bright and beautifully maintained. They were designed in the 1860's by the well-known Victorian garden designer William Nesfield and his son, Markham. As you stroll down the broad path you will notice two forces at play; there are the colourful spring and summer bedding plants with avenues of trees and evergreen hedges and there is also the informality of the English garden, which is planted in raised beds to the side of the walk. The two create an attractive environment with 24 garden ornaments, including eight recently restored fountains. The avenue of trees continues along the Broad Walk to the north of Chester Road with large chestnuts and London planes and a foxglove tree at the southern end.

With its rolling lawns, large rose garden, secret gardens, woods and lakes, Regent's Park caters for many different moods. Surrounding palatial terraces, the fabulous sights and sounds emanating from the southern edge of London Zoo and the many herbaceous borders all make it somewhere full of surprise and colour.

RICHMOND PARK   *See illustration 4, between pages 32 and 33*

Address: Richmond, Surrey TW10; **Tel**: 020 8948 3209; **Owner**: The Royal Parks; **Location**: Between Richmond, Wimbledon, Kingston upon Thames & Twickenham; **Transport**: Richmond tube (District Line) & train station; Bus 72,74,85,371; **Entrance**: Free; **Opening Times**: Summer 7am-dusk; winter 7.30am-dusk; **Other Information**: Cafe, deer herds, disabled access, dogs welcome, events, parking, toilets; **Seasonal Features**: January, February, April, May, June, July, August, September, October; heather garden, camellias, azaleas, rhododendrons, rose garden, autumnal trees

This is the largest park in London covering an area of about 2,500 acres. It has a wild character and a sweeping, hilly landscape with grassland, woods and gardens from which, on a fine day, you can clearly see St Paul's Cathedral – over twelve miles away.

In 1625 Charles I retreated to the country at Richmond to distance himself from the plague in London. He established private hunting grounds there by walling off a large area of land by the river. Nearly 400 years on, this open land is wholly engulfed by the sprawling city of London. Plantations were originally laid for shooting and timber production though in 1904 the shooting ended and they, like the rest of the park, were opened to the public and have since been maintained for aesthetic value.

For the visitor today the large park is refreshingly bleak and open. Herds of deer graze and rut among the stands of bracken or shelter under the ancient oaks. A prehistoric burial mound, probably dating from the Bronze Age, lies on the summit of a hill on the north west of the park. It is worth visiting this to experience the wonderful views down the snaking Thames or across to Windsor Castle – thirteen miles away. In the other direction you can look towards central London and spot various landmarks. The other fine viewpoint in Richmond Park is at Pembroke Lodge, where you can also purchase refreshments and relax on the lawn surrounded by displays of roses and bedding plants.

A real treasure to be discovered here is the Isabella Plantation which is a wooded garden enclosed in 1831. Many grand trees such as oaks and beeches are mixed with more exotic and showy magnolias, camellias, witch hazels, spindles and azaleas. There is a lovely heather garden, a bog garden, an acer glade and a camellia walk and a lively stream flows through the centre linking two ponds which contain yellow flag irises. From April to June the rhododendrons and azaleas in the Isabella Plantation are spectacular. In April primulas around the pond are in flower and in May bluebells bloom in the wood, which is a renowned bird sanctuary. It is also worth visiting in autumn as the maples and oaks have a show to give.

Although Isabella in spring may be its principal glory in the eyes of many, Richmond Park is an important resource all year for Londoners. You will find nowhere better in the city really to clear your head than this wonderfully open and beautiful landscape, so unchanged over time.

ROOKERY GARDENS

Address: The Rookery, Streatham Common South, London SW16; **Tel**: 020 7926 9334; **Owner**: Lambeth Borough Council; **Location**: On top of Streatham Common; **Transport**: Streatham train station; Bus 249; **Entrance**: Free; **Opening Times**: Daily, except 25th Dec, 9am-dusk; **Other Information**: Cafe, disabled access, dogs on lead on top terrace only, parking, picnic area, toilets; **Seasonal Features**: May, June, July, August; old english garden, rock garden, white garden, orchard, herbaceous borders

Make your way up to the top end of Streatham Common and your efforts will be rewarded with a fine garden to visit and sweeping views to gaze upon. The Rookery Garden is peaceful and well-maintained and includes a burgeoning old english garden, a secluded rock garden and a white garden which looks at its best in June and July. There is also an orchard with a picnic area and a high terrace garden containing rhododendrons and lilacs and many benches, where you can relax while looking down across the garden or cityscape.

The walled old english garden is a sheltered and delightful mix of fragrance and colour. Yews, variegated hollies, cherries, apple and gorse give height and winter structure while the flowering season lasts from early spring to late autumn with a jostling mixture of perennials and annual bedding plants. Outer beds are stocked with brightly coloured annuals surrounding yuccas while the central herbaceous bed is stocked with plants such as sunflowers, rudbeckia, foxgloves, geraniums, lavender, solidago, asters, echinops, delphiniums and potentilla. Amongst the floral profusion in the old english garden you may find a sundial and a well which dates from 1659 – one of three original wells belonging to the old house for which this was the walled garden. There is a rose arbour and at one end a round lily pond encircled by clipped yews and climbing wisteria, roses and ivy.

Adjacent to the old english garden lies a small rose bed and annual bedding, again overhung by some impressive wisteria. A white garden has been laid out along the bottom of the slope which contains an interesting mix of herbs, shrubs and climbers and variegated-leaved plants such as hollies, euonymus and ivies.

Two further sections of the garden remain – the old orchard and the rock garden. The orchard is set aside for picnics and contains an attractive hedge of variegated holly along one side as well as some interesting autumnal trees such as the ginkgo, maple and golden rain tree. The extensive rock garden is a peaceful haven with a stream running briskly through it. Ferns, Japanese acers, heathers, irises, gunnera, a large corkscrew willow and a goldfish pond all help to ensure year-round colour and interest. With all the seasonal botanical treats provided by its constituent parts there should be something for everyone at the Rookery.

ROOTS & SHOOTS

Address: The Vauxhall Centre, Walnut Tree Walk, London SE11; **Tel**: 020 7587 1131;
Owner: Lambeth Borough Council; **Transport**: Lambeth North tube (Bakerloo Line);
Bus 3,159,344,C10; **Entrance**: Free; **Opening Times**: Garden centre: May & June,
Mon-Fri 9.30am-4pm, Sat 10am-2pm; July-April, Mon-Fri 1.30pm-4pm; Wildlife garden:
open on appt. by tel; **Other Information**: No dogs in wildlife garden, plant sales May
& June, courses for disadvantaged young people; **Seasonal Features**: May, June, July;
wildlife garden with summer meadow, wild flowers and shrub roses

Just down from the Imperial War Museum in South London is a small,
enthusiastic and hard-working band of people with a very commendable
fight on their hands. It is a battle that could continue indefinitely but one
can already see from the results that the fighters and nature have made a
remarkable start. The challenge, since 1982, has been to take a derelict Civil
Defence site and create Roots & Shoots – a diverse, attractive and peaceful
wildlife garden with a garden centre and an office running practical and
educational courses for the local community. What was once an extremely
drear, overgrown and polluted patch of land has been transformed into a
thriving, colourful and lush garden with a range of different habitats, while
the centre provides essential training for disadvantaged young people. In
1998 they had a 70% success rate in finding retail, gardening and
maintenance jobs for their trainees.

Roots & Shoots is an oasis of colour and beauty in one of the more
deprived areas of London. Its wildlife garden contains a pond, large
summer meadow, walnut coppice, hop hedge, thyme lawn and a
Mediterranean mound. There are also beehives and butterfly borders which
allow local children to interact with nature at first hand and the London
Beekeeper's Association runs courses here. The shrub roses and meadow
are attractive in late spring and early summer and the small thyme lawn
is a blur of pink and white when it blooms in June. From native spring
bulbs and summer flowers, herbs, shrubs and climbers such as kiwi fruits
through to other notables such as the Japanese horse chestnut, pampas
grass and bulrushes around the pond, a haze of colour and form awaits you
in this hidden, diverse and secluded paradise.

To book a visit to the wildlife garden you should telephone the Centre
on 020 7582 1800. For pre-arranged groups there can be activities laid on
including pond dipping and mini beast hunts; for the most part, however,
it is the thriving project and the beauty of nature, as it blossoms in all its

mid-summer glory on a patch of land once nothing but a rubbish tip, that is enjoyable to see and worthy to support.

ROYAL BOTANIC GARDENS, KEW

See illustrations 6 and 11, between pages 32 and 33, and 18, 21 and 22, between pages 96 and 97

Address: Kew, Richmond, Surrey TW9; Tel: 020 8940 1171; **Owner**: Trustees of the Royal Botanic Gardens; **Location**: West of Kew Road; **Transport**: Kew Gardens tube (District Line) & train station; Bus 65,391; Boats to Kew Gardens Pier; **Entrance**: Entrance charge; **Opening Times**: Daily, winter 9.30am-5.30pm, later in summer; **Other Information**: Cafe, disabled access, guide dogs only, events, guided tours, museum, parking, restaurant, shop, toilets; **Seasonal Features**: January, February, March, April, May, June, July, August, September, October, November, December; Alpine House, autumnal trees, azaleas, bamboos, berberis dell, bluebells, camellias, cherry blossom, crocus lawn, Evolution House, formal bedding, grass garden, heathers, holly walk, Japanese garden, lilacs, laburnum alley, magnolias, nosegay garden, orchid festival, Palm House, Queen's garden, rock garden, rose garden, rhododendron dell, secluded garden, Temperate House, waterlilies

These intriguingly beautiful world famous gardens hold over 35,000 different types of plants and whatever time of year you visit you will find much to marvel at. The gardens cover 300 acres along the south bank of the Thames with scenic views across to Syon House. They contain many interesting buildings which document their rich history from the original Kew Palace built in for the Royals in 1631 to the Princess of Wales Conservatory opened in 1984. Sir William Chambers designed the glasshouses and buildings in the original Royal Botanic Gardens as well as the elegant oriental pagoda which was erected in the 1760s, a majestic-scale folly indeed.

Visit the Royal Botanic Gardens on a sunny spring or summer day and it is tempting to wander the lawns soaking up the bold Kew Palace, the elegant glasshouses and the borders, dells and avenues of herbaceous plants, shrubs and stately trees. There is an azalea garden and a rhododendron dell with a magnificent spreading London plane tree which both look at their most colourful in May and June. The bamboo garden has year round interest, as do the order beds and Japanese garden which contains an extremely ornate Japanese Gateway, a copy of the Gateway of the Imperial Messenger, the entrance to a Buddhist Temple in Kyoto.

The more wild and naturalised part of the gardens in which you are most likely to lose yourself, is the south west end, furthest from the main gate. At the far end of the lake there is a fine view across the river to Syon Park and then the paths become more sparse and delve into a peaceful pinetum surrounding Queen Charlotte's Cottage, a thatched lodge built in 1772. The main attraction of this area is every spring when it becomes a sea of blue as millions of bluebells flower around the cottage glade. The result is spectacular, if crowded. For the rest of the year it is somewhat under-visited and for the keen plantsman there are some interesting trees to be sought out in the adjacent arboretum.

At the heart of the gardens is the mesmeric Victorian Palm House. This amazing wrought iron and glass creation was designed by Richard Turner and opened in 1848 when visitors flocked to see it and the newly discovered 'exotics' within. Today you can view mature coconut palms, a royal palm and a giant bamboo which all reach the palm house roof and must pose some problems for the building's managers. The world's oldest pot plant, an encephalartos species, was planted in 1775 and resides at one end of the Palm House, while in the basement is an impressive aquarium with seaweed, coral reef fish and sea horses. The rose garden behind the Palm House is a summer feature and vistas run both west and south to the Thames and intriguing pagoda.

Among the buildings still to explore is the temperate glasshouse which is among the world's largest greenhouses. It was designed by Decimus Burton in 1860 and contains plants from Australia, New Zealand and South Africa arranged geographically. There are informative labels and colourful climbers as well as a cool central stream and pond. Dominating the main section is the towering Chilean wine palm which was grown from seed in 1846 and now stands over 17 metres tall. An evolution house nearby will cater for your primeval instincts while for those with an interest in man's achievements with plants there is the recently restored museum of economic botany by the palm house pond. There are also no less than 800 stunning botanical oil paintings by Marianne North in her gallery to be marvelled at and several places in the gardens at which you can relax with a drink.

Highlights of the Royal Botanic Gardens, and there are many, include the woodland garden, holly walk, strawberry trees, camellias and heathers at the start of the year followed by the rock garden, snowdrops and carpet of six million crocuses in February. Cherry blossom, forsythia and an orchid festival feature in March, while the bluebells, magnolias, azaleas and rhododendrons steal the show in mid to late spring. The displays of summer bedding, herbaceous borders, rose garden, Queen's garden, grass garden and waterlilies all look spectacular for summer. In autumn many maples, chestnuts and liquidambars in the woodland areas give eye-catching displays and in winter months the alpine house, winter-flowering shrubs and little heather garden come into bloom. For the plantsman all 70,000 or so plant species are labelled and for those who just want to roam and be amazed the Royal Botanic Gardens at Kew is the place to be.

ROYAL HOSPITAL GARDENS, CHELSEA (RANELAGH GARDENS)

Address: Royal Hospital Road, London SW3; **Tel**: 020 7730 0161; **Owner**: Royal Hospital Chelsea; **Location**: Entrance gate on Royal Hospital Road ; **Transport**: Sloane Square tube (District & Circle Lines); Bus 239, 137; **Entrance**: Free; **Opening Times**: Daily, except 25th Dec. & May and June due to Chelsea Flower Show,10am-12.45pm & 2pm-sunset (Sun 2pm-sunset); **Other Information**: Disabled access, no dogs, toilets; **Seasonal Features**: September, October; autumnal trees

On entering the gates of the Royal Chelsea Hospital you will usually be greeted by a friendly Chelsea Pensioner. In their traditional scarlet coats or blue shirt sleeves the Pensioners are very much in evidence around the gardens along with the public and can be found lounging on outdoor benches or manning the Royal Hospital Museum. The Royal Hospital itself is bold and rambling. It was founded by King Charles II in 1682 as a retreat for veterans of the regular army who were either wounded or unfit for duty after more than 20 years' active service. The building was designed by Sir Christopher Wren who entrusted the layout of the grounds to George London and Henry Wise – fashionable garden designers of the late 17th century.

The Ranelagh Gardens are somewhat timeless and grandiose with their collection of aged trees as well as the formal lawns around the Royal Hospital containing rose and lavender beds. Between the Hospital and the river is a large flat area of lawn with a central war memorial on which the annual Chelsea Flower Show is held. There were originally swanneries here where the royal birds were reared for life on the river. You are welcome to walk here and view the Hospital South Terrace Court and a regimental avenue of London planes reaching down the eastern flank.

Ranelagh Gardens run parallel to Chelsea Bridge Road but are well screened from it by mature trees including a large blue gum, false hickory, weeping willow and ash, acer, tree of heaven, maidenhair tree, magnolia and snakebark maple. Many of these give lovely splashes of autumn colour amongst the well kept lawns and there is a summerhouse near the entrance with a tree map.

You can wander round long stretches of peaceful, undulating lawns where large evergreens and hollies will provide you with privacy and solitude. Raised mounds of trees and shrubs are remnants of a pleasure garden that was once considered among the most fashionable in the country. In the 18th century a magnificent rotunda, 185 ft, in diameter, was the central feature but the garden later deteriorated and was used for food cultivation and Pensioners' allotments before its restoration along the designs of the original late 17th century creation.

ROYAL INSTITUTE OF BRITISH ARCHITECTS (RIBA) GARDEN

Address: 66 Portland Place, London W1N; **Tel**: 020 7631 0467; **Owner**: Royal Institute of British Architects; **Location**: First Floor Roof Terrace; **Transport**: Great Portland Street tube (Circle, Metropolitan & Hamm. & City Lines) & Regent's Park tube (Bakerloo Line); Bus 135, C2; **Entrance**: Free; **Opening Times**: Mon-Fri 8am-6pm, Sat 8am-5pm; **Other Information**: Bookshop, no dogs, programme of architectural exhibitions, restaurant, toilets; **Seasonal Features**: January, February, November, December; sculpture-fountain by William Pye, topiary yews, ferns, hostas, birch trees

On the first floor terrace of the Royal Institute of British Architects' building you will encounter a small roof garden planted in tall, shiny metal containers. Designed by Elsie Josland and Helen McCabe, it was opened in September 1998 and incorporates a striking sculpture-fountain by William Pye titled 'Water Trellis' which is switched off on dull days.

The garden has been cleverly planted with soft, dark, textural foliage which contrasts well with the bright metal of the containers and modern fountain. Topiary yews, hostas, hemp agrimony and some unusual ferns all flourish and in the centre a pair of tubs hold sizeable birch trees. Violets, white impatiens and irises all add splashes of colour and are dotted evenly around. A restaurant, the *Patisserie Valerie* (Tel. 020 7631 0467), occupies the terrace garden and its chrome seats and tables blend in well with the planters, allowing diners to relax amidst the feathery foliage and enjoy the variety of botanical textures and shapes around them.

ST JAMES'S PARK   *See illustration 1, between pages 32 and 33*

Address: Westminster, London SW1A; **Owner**: The Royal Parks; **Location**: Between The Mall, Birdcage Walk & Horse Guards Parade; **Transport**: St James's Park tube

(District & Circle Lines); Bus 2,8,9,14,16,19,22,38,52,73,82; **Entrance**: Free; **Opening Times**: Daily, 5am-midnight; **Other Information**: Bandstand, cafe, children's playground, disabled access, dogs on leads only, events, toilets; **Seasonal Features**: May, June, July, August, September, October; cherry blossom, roses, herbaceous borders, autumn crocuses, autumnal trees, hostas

This small but attractive park is one of London's oldest, dating back to the 1530's when Henry VIII made an enclosure there for deer coursing. It has always had a strong link with Royalty and now has a prominent position linking both Buckingham Palace and St James's with the intriguing Gothic edifice by Horse Guards Parade and the old Palace of Westminster.

It was the French garden designer, Le Notre, who in 1660 drew up the original plans for St James's Park for Charles II. One and a half centuries later John Nash was engaged by George IV to redesign the park and gave us a more curvaceous lake and randomly-spaced trees and flower beds.

The park's central lake is actually a canal and is home to numerous wildfowl such as the rather comical pelicans which have been a feature since the 17th century. As you stroll round the lake being entertained by feathered residents and glimpsing majestic buildings you will come across some interesting flowers and trees. Around the Queen Victoria Memorial outside Buckingham Palace are some colourful displays of bedding plants worth a detour in spring and summer. Also near the Palace you will find some interesting herbaceous borders with an emphasis on texture and aroma and rose beds flowering in June and July. In autumn a mass of little autumn crocuses paint the ground by Marlborough Gate which leads on to The Mall with its stately rows of London plane trees. There is much autumnal leaf and fruit colour in St James's such as on the maidenhair tree and twisted old mulberry at the east end next to Duck Island. This island acts as a refuge for the wildfowl and an attractive garden surrounds its guardian's house, Duck Island Cottage. From here you can admire the turrets and spires surrounding Horse Guards Parade, contemplate the Guards Memorial or stop for refreshment at the Cake House cafe where you will find a large fountain jet.

The other side of the lake is quieter and more shady and you are less likely to be disturbed if you just want to have some peace. It holds shrubberies and flowerbeds to be explored beneath the spreading London planes. St James's is a popular, attractive little park with style and a touch of pomp. It is planted for a long flowering season and there are free band performances on most summer days in the bandstand by The Mall.

ST JOHN'S WOOD CHURCH BURIAL GROUND

Address: Wellington Road, London NW8; **Tel:** 020 7641 5271; **Owner:** Westminster City Council; **Transport:** St John's Wood tube (Jubilee Line); Bus 13,82,113,274; **Entrance:** Free; **Opening Times:** Daily, Mon-Sat 8am-dusk, Sun & Bank Hols 9am-dusk; **Other Information:** Children's playground, dogs on leads only, nature reserve; **Seasonal Features:** April, May, June, July; cherry blossom, formal bedding, wild flowers,

St John's Wood Church Burial Ground was used as a burial ground from 1814-1855 when there were recorded to be some 50,000 graves there. It is still consecrated ground, but is no longer used as a burial site, and is instead a popular public park with well managed gardens and local nature reserve important for many species.

There is some colourful, formal bedding by the church where a line of Kanzan cherries, which screen the gardens from a busy roundabout, produce a blossom bouquet in May. As well as the beds of spring and summer bedding plants there are herbaceous beds with mahonias, red-hot pokers, cannas and other lilies. All seem well cared for and there are plenty of benches for visitors.

For those wanting to stretch their legs there is a small park which is largely shady with some sunny glades containing more shrub and flower borders. Some interesting trees include the Norwegian maple, Turkey oak, weeping ash and an avenue of whitebeam. The graves are grouped in several of the quieter sites in the park and add a more sombre atmosphere to your visit. One area is set aside as a local nature reserve with buddleia, hawthorn, lavender, red campion and bluebells. Butterflies, goldfinches and bats are all at home there.

Elsewhere you can find a drinking fountain, a children's play area and some interesting tombs and memorials and you will find this spacious garden contains a good mixture of leafy overhanging trees and well-maintained lawns and flower beds.

ST MICHAEL'S CONVENT GARDEN

National Garden Scheme (NGS): see note on p30

Address: St Michael's Convent, 56 Ham Common, Richmond, Surrey TW10; **Owner:** Community of the Sisters of the Church; **Location:** North side of Ham Common; **Transport:** Richmond tube (District Line); Bus 65; **Opening Times:** NGS open days only (see NGS book); **Other Information:** Guide dogs only; **Seasonal Features:** Bible Garden, herbaceous borders, meditation garden, orchards, working kitchen garden

For a sheltered and peaceful garden that is both lush and lovingly cared for you should make time to visit St Michael's Convent in Ham when it annually opens its four-acre secret garden to the public under the National Gardens Scheme. The convent stands serenely on the northern edge of Ham Common and houses the busy Community of the Sisters of the Church, an Anglican Order founded in 1870. Within the front yard magnolias, Judas trees, very old yews and a giant oak help set the atmosphere of quiet reflection which the Community strives for

This is a fine example of a garden that provides constant fun, food, relaxation and work for many people and contains interest and variety for visitors. Its large, walled kitchen garden is meticulously kept and includes fruit trees, fragrant herbs and three greenhouses. In one of these you will find grape vines and in another a collection of cacti lingers. Venture on through to the old orchard and you will encounter a white border and beds of soft fruits which lead up to the Cottage and Bible Gardens. The Bible Garden is a small plot containing many of the plants mentioned in the Bible such as lily, bay, rosemary, poppy, rose and even thorns. An accompanying handbook can be purchased from the convent. The little Circle Garden nestling beside the Bible Garden is meant for meditation and you may like to rest quietly on a bench sheltered by evergreens and look out across the garden's circular paths which symbolise circles of prayer.

The rest of the northern end of the garden is taken up by expansive orchard and prayer wood edged by wild areas along which you will find benches and can peacefully enjoy the ambience. Some of the fruit trees are old and gnarled and much of the grass is left to grow long to encourage wildlife. You can also find a pond, a summer house and a hermitage. The final and most formal part of the garden is the large lawn behind the convent which is sided by two colourful herbaceous borders. Two rose arbours and rockeries fill one corner of the lawn while a 300-year-old mulberry tree gives the garden an air of stability to soothe even the most troubled and restless of moods.

SYON PARK   *See illustrations 8 and 9, between pages 32 and 33*

Address: Brentford, Middlesex TW8; **Tel**: 020 8560 0881; **Owner**: The Duke of Northumberland; **Location**: North bank of the River Thames, opposite Kew Gardens; **Transport**: Gunnersbury tube (District Line); Kew Bridge train station; Bus 237,267; **Entrance**: Entrance charge; **Opening Times**: Gardens open daily, except 25, 26 Dec, 10am-5.30pm (dusk if earlier); House open 17 Mar-30 Oct, Wed, Thur, Sun & Bank

Syon Park

Hols, 11am-5pm; **Other Information**:Aquatic experience, art centre, butterfly house, cafe, children's playground, disabled access, dogs welcome in parkland only, events, garden centre, parking, shop, toilets, trout fishery; **Seasonal Features**:April, May, June, July, September, October; cherry blossom, wild flowers, azaleas, rhododendrons, rose garden, water garden, autumnal trees, conservatory

Syon Park, owned by the Duke of Northumberland and dating from the 1540's, is one of the oldest landscapes in the country. It contains more than 3,000 trees – one in every four of which is over 100 years old; an impressive one in seven is over 200. Syon House itself is a Tudor monument built on the site of a medieval abbey dissolved by Henry VIII in 1539. In the mid 18th century Robert Adam created some of his finest interiors at Syon House and Capability Brown laid out two lakes in the magnificent 200 acre park and garden.

In the garden today the wings and curvaceous dome of the great conservatory rise up to greet you. Enter this and you will find a fern-cloaked waterfall, cacti, bedding plants and climbers and then be led on through to a formal Italian garden with clipped yew bushes and a pond. Return through the looming conservatory and 55 acres of informal garden wait to be explored including a large lake and rose garden with spectacular views across the tidal meadows between Syon House and the Thames. Peacocks and a miniature railway serve as added attractions, while for plant enthusiasts there are over 200 species of rare trees, including stately specimens of the pagoda tree and black pine as well as some exotic oaks.

On a meander around the garden lake you will encounter an open lawn with well-stocked herbaceous beds overlooked by a Doric column bearing a motherly statue of Flora, Goddess of Flowers. To one side of this a small footbridge leads to a wild flower meadow, in bloom from March to May, when it is a haven for butterflies, and from where it is pleasant to gaze back across the lake at Flora's Lawn. Crossing back to the north of the lake, there is still a water garden with a tumbling stream and a shady woodland walk with yet more ancient trees to be sought out. In spring this last is awash with colour as azaleas and rhododendrons steal the show; and in autumn it is worth the walk in order not to miss the fiery autumnal foliage of trees such as liquidambars and maples. You can now complete a full circuit of the beautifully sculpted lake with weeping willows, Caucasian wing nuts, gunnera, and pampas grass clumps brushing its banks. Syon Park holds a leisurely air, and many diversions and makes a very pleasant escape from urbanity from April to October.

THAMES BARRIER PARK

Address: Barrier Point Road, London E16; **Tel**: 020 7511 4111; **Owner**: London Development Agency; **Location**: North bank of Thames, between North Woolwich Road and the Thames Barrier; **Transport**: Canning Town tube (Jubilee Line), Canning Town DLR station, Silvertown train station; Bus 69,474; **Entrance**: Free; **Opening Times**: Dawn-dusk; **Other Information**: Café, disabled access, dogs welcome, riverside walk, parking, toilets; **Seasonal Features**: April, May, June, July, August; fountain plaza (summer only), geraniums, herbaceous borders, hydrangeas, irises, lavender, sunken garden, wildflowers

The Thames Barrier Park is sited on an old Petroleum and Chemical Works that once operated from Prince Regents Wharf in the Royal Docks. If one goes back more than 150 years, it was probably undeveloped riverbank. Today's award-winning park is part of a programme of regeneration for the Docklands and Thames Gateway and it now rewards its visitors with a lively fountain plaza, a large sheltered sunken garden, or 'green dock', and spacious lawns featuring colour-themed wildflower meadows.

From anywhere in the park the huge stainless steel shells of the Thames Barrier rise up from the riverward end. These house mighty hydraulic power packs that raise and lower massive gates and thereby tame the river's tidal surges. From the riverside promenade you can peacefully survey the whole spectrum of city and river life from shy shore birds to old industrial warehouses and the giant modern towers of Canary Wharf. The past is reflected in the park's layout with the central sunken garden positioned at right angles to the river in place of a Victorian dock. Long strips of undulating yew hedges run the length of the garden and contrast well with the seasonal rainbow effect produced by its many colourful shrubs and herbaceous plants. As the herbaceous planting is in large blocks, the garden's sheltered paths are particularly fragrant in mid summer when the colours are most intense. Dreamy lavender leads to vivid rudbeckias, to deep blue agapanthus to blazing lilies. The walls of this 'green dock' are embedded with *Lonicera nitida* and above it walkways and bridges are shaped to recall dockside cranes.

The sunken garden runs the whole length of the park from its river promenade to a fountain plaza at the northern end. During the summer, the latter is a vivacious display with 32 fountains constantly rising from a stone courtyard, floodlit at night. On either side of the garden expansive lawns each contain wildflower meadows which flush with colour every spring. Clumps of healthy young oak, birch and pine trees will bring more

wildlife to these areas as they grow and a grid of hornbeam hedges with
blocks of beech gives structure to the lawns. The park is shielded from the
sunken car park to the north by a bamboo screen and from the residential
developments on either side by shrub borders. On lawn adjoining the
riverside walk the Pavilion of Remembrance quietly commemorates East
Londoners who died in the Blitz. Its design is based on a traditional Mogul
garden and it features a roof on slender 26ft high poles with stone benches
below. Both here and in the park's visitor pavilion, which is an oak framed
teahouse with etched glass, are pleasant places to sit and contemplate the
past life of the area that is now subtly incorporated into this green haven.

TIBETAN PEACE GARDEN (SAMTEN KYIL)

Address: Geraldine Mary Harmsworth Park, Kennington, London SE I I; **Tel**: 020 7404
2889; **Owner**: Tibet Foundation; **Location**: By the Imperial War Museum; **Transport**:
Lambeth North tube (Bakerloo Line); Bus 344, C I 0; **Entrance**: Free; **Opening Times**:
Daily; **Other Information**: Guide dogs only, guide available in Museum reception;
Seasonal Features: January, February, March, October, November, December; cherry
blossom, birches, contemporary sculpture

The Tibetan Peace Garden is positioned symbolically alongside the
grandiose Imperial War Museum with a pair of huge naval guns pointing
threateningly towards the gate. The garden was opened by His Holiness
the Dalai Lama in May 1999 and is funded by the Tibet Foundation, which
aims to further the understanding of Tibetan Buddhism and encourage
world peace. The sculptor/designer is Hamish Horsley and the overall
design strives to bring together contemporary western imagery with
traditional Tibetan culture.

   At the entrance of the garden the tone of the area is set by a Language
Pillar of Portland stone which carries the Dalai Lama's message of peace
and harmony in four languages. The garden itself is a round construction
based on a fundamental Buddhist image, the Wheel of Time, and contains
a circular arbour enclosing icons and beds of plants from Tibet and the
Himalayas. The western world is represented by four impressive Portland
stone sculptures symbolising air, fire, earth and water while spiritual
Tibetan icons include a circular bronze *Mandala*, a Buddhist symbol believed
to have the power to confer blessings on all who see it. This forms the
garden's centrepiece and is surrounded by more classic Buddhist images,
the 'Eight Auspicious Symbols'. Low contemplation seats also encircle the

revered *Mandala* and provide somewhere quietly to rest, backed by flower beds and protected by the surrounding leafy pergola.

The path leading from the Language Pillar to the garden is bordered by white roses and a bed immediately exterior to the circular garden contains potentilla, poppies, clematis, honeysuckle and jasmine. The modern sculptures and pale stone are complemented by a blue and white colour scheme and on the outside lawn cherries, silver birches, oaks and large London plane trees serve both to provide colour from spring to autumn and to screen the busy road system. Outer shrubberies will grow thicker and taller in time and in the neat and spiritual peace garden all is still whilst the traffic races by outside the perimeter fence.

TRENT COUNTRY PARK

Address: Cockfosters Road, Enfield EN1; **Tel**: 020 8449 8706; **Owner**: London Borough of Enfield; **Location**: Bounded by Cockfosters Road (A111), Hadley Road and Enfield Road); **Transport**: Cockfosters & Oakwood tubes (Piccadilly Line); Enfield Chase train station; Bus 121,298,299,307,384; Entrance: Free; **Opening Times**: Daily, dawn-dusk (traffic 8am-dusk); **Other Information**: Animal corner, bike trail, cafe, car park, disabled access, dogs welcome, equestrian centre, fishing, golf course, nature trail, shop, sports facilities, toilets, visitor centre; **Seasonal Features**: March, April, May, June, September, October; daffodils, wisteria, rhododendrons, autumnal trees

In a valuable stretch of rolling countryside protected by London's Green Belt lies an old garden with some glorious, seasonal floral displays. Trent Country Park is located between Cockfosters and Oakwood Underground stations and is just a 5 minute walk from the latter. It is an immense 413 acres in size and contains woodland, farmland and a golf course as well as landscaped lakes, avenues and vistas and a 14th century moat.

The park has formerly been both a Royal hunting forest and a private estate with expansive grounds. At its heart is a grand house which was built in the 1920s by its last private owner, Sir Philip Sassoon. He was also reponsible for erecting a huge and elegant obelisk in the north of the park and for planting thousands of daffodils around the house that still form a marvellous spectacle for the visitors of today. During World War II, Trent Park was requisitioned by the War Office and afterwards the Ministry of Education took over the house as an emergency teacher training centre. In 1951 Middlesex County Council compulsorily purchased the entire Trent Park estate to safeguard the Green Belt and the house and surrounding buildings were occupied by Middlesex University which remains there today. The present park opened to the public in 1973 providing large areas of mature deciduous woodland with well marked footpaths and bike trails and open green spaces with many sports facilities.

A double avenue of lime trees leads from the car park to the old house and here you can rest on the front terrace to admire views across the rolling lawns, and lakes, up to the towering obelisk. In March daffodils carpet the southern lawns and in May you should not miss the flowering of the wonderful wisteria walk tucked away on the hillside to the east of the main house. There is also a colourful spring display of rhododendrons and azaleas along the walk leading up to the obelisk as well as in the old water and woodland gardens located beside the lakes. Autumn is an evocative season for a walk here with many fiery reds and golds, and abundant nuts and fruits in the acres of mixed, mature woodland.

TRINITY HOSPICE GARDENS National Garden Scheme (NGS): see note on page 30

Address: 30 Clapham Common North Side, London SW4; **Tel**: 020 7787 1000; **Owner**: Trinity Hospice; **Location**: Clapham Common North Side; **Transport**: Clapham Common tube (Northern Line); Clapham Junction train station; Bus 35,37,137; **Opening Times**: NGS open days only (see NGS book); **Other Information**: Guide dogs only, plant sales; **Seasonal Features**: Spring bulbs, cherry blossom, herbaceous borders

If you venture away from Clapham Common and behind the Trinity Hospice on Clapham Common North Side you will find yourself in a quiet garden where the pace of life slows, water laps away the time in an attractive modern fountain and sweet herbal fragrances fill the air.

The garden twists and turns over nearly two acres encompassing a croquet lawn, a wild flower area, a peaceful lily pond, a large formal lawn, a terrace and well-stocked spring and summer herbaceous borders. It was designed by John Medhurst and restored by Lanning Roper's friends as his memorial. There are some well-rounded, mature trees including two large mulberries, a magnificent horse chestnut, a catalpa, a swamp cypress and several cherries – one of which is a designated Blessing Tree and is hung with personalised blessings inscribed on copper tags. Much is in flower in mid spring when the apple blossom, wisteria, lilacs, primroses, fritillaries and cowslips are all on show.

Space, peace and time are all in abundance here and if you explore you will find a sitting circle engulfed in the soft pastel shades of roses, pink lavender, nepeta, salvia and buddleia. Paths wander around shrubberies, across lawns, through pergolas and lead you to a hidden wild garden containing a lily pond with a modern sculpture by the American artist George Rickey balanced delicately above the water. Where better to relax with your cup of tea and enjoy a beautiful garden.

VICTORIA AND ALBERT MUSEUM GARDEN (PIRELLI GARDEN)

Address: Cromwell Road, London SW7; **Tel**: 020 7942 2000; **Owner**: Victoria and Albert Museum; **Location**: Inner Museum Courtyard; **Transport**: South Kensington tube (District & Circle Lines); Bus 14,74,C1; **Entrance**: Free **Opening Times**: Daily, except 24-26 Dec, 10am-5.45pm, Wed and last Fri of month 10am-10pm. Garden closed when raining; **Other Information**: Cafe, disabled access, guide dogs only, gallery talks & tours, shop, toilets; **Seasonal Features**: May, June, July, August, September, October; incense cedars, fountain, autumnal trees

Visit this handsome, Italianate garden endowed with a magnificent space in the inner sanctum of the Victoria and Albert Museum and you will be inspired by the world's greatest museum of art and design.

The Pirelli Garden lies at the heart of the Museum complex and is distinguished by its Vulcan fountain and the magnificent architecture that surrounds it. The side facing the door, having been the original entrance to the Museum, is particularly spectacular. Its Italianate columns and recessed arches are decorated with intricate terracotta and mosaic, celebrating the origins of the V&A in the Great Exhibition. There are surrounding images of the seven ages of man and statues of the Museum's founders. The garden itself has a classic geometrical design with a large, central fountain and formal rows of incense cedars planted in a stepped arrangement on raised lawns. These trees have a columnar habit and in the urban environment of South Kensington grow no higher than 60 feet. There are two opposing groves of Italian alders that are lighter and more open than the cedars, and complement the shady southern side of the quadrangle.

The central path between the two raised lawns and around the elegant vulcan fountain is paved in York stone which complements the terracotta of the surrounding buildings. The great portico facade of the mid-Victorian elevation rears up immediately behind the Pirelli Garden exuberantly displaying arches, columns, alcoves, etc. and the garden's stark simplicity provides a refreshing counterpoint to the overwrought decoration. During the summer months you can enjoy the tranquil surroundings of the garden cafe and in Autumn 2004, the area will be redesigned to refresh the existing landscape and so continue to provide an elegant Italianate garden where visitors can relax at the heart of the V and A.

VICTORIA PARK

Address:Victoria Park Road, London E2; **Owner**:Tower Hamlets Borough; **Transport**: Mile End tube (Central & District Lines); Bus 8,277,333,D6; **Entrance**: Free; **Opening Times**: 8am-8.30pm or dusk; **Other Information**:Animal enclosure, bandstand, cafe, children's playground, disabled access, dogs welcome outside the old english garden, sports facilities, toilets; **Seasonal Features**: April, May, June, July, August; old english garden, hollies, bluebells, cherry blossom, formal bedding, rose garden

Victoria Park is one of London's oldest parks. It was opened in 1848 after 30,000 local residents signed a petition to Queen Victoria asking her to create the first Royal Park in East London. It had been reported that the mortality rate was higher in the East End than elsewhere in the City and it was thought that a large open space would dilute the polluted air and reduce disease. Victoria Park was designed by the popular 19th century garden designer James Pennethorne, and completed in 1850 and has since been the venue for many political rallies and social occasions. It fell into a state of some neglect during the present century but in 1986 it underwent a multi-million pound restoration project, and you can now once again sense its past grandeur as you explore its rolling grounds.

In the southern end of the park a large lake is enhanced by a large rose border, a cascade, an elegant fountain and two islands shelter a busy Canada goose and coot population. A cafe is located in a pavilion on the bank where it is pleasant to sit and view the scene. Around the opposite edge of the lake grasses, herbaceous borders and hanging floral baskets give bright splashes of summer colour. An avenue of spring-flowering cherry trees runs north up to a shrubbery and a children's play area by Royal Gate East. There is also a bluebell wood which acquires a carpet of blue in May.

Grove Road runs from north to south through Victoria Park and on the eastern side is more open with a large lido field, tennis courts, a bowling green, cricket pitch and sports ground. There are long avenues of old trees and quite a bit of land to cover in between attractions. There is also a series of lakes, an adventure playground, an old english garden, a bandstand and a very substantial Memorial Drinking Fountain surrounded by colourful floral bedding. The old english garden has been sited next to the adventure playground and tends to be used as an extension of it, which can spoil the atmosphere. However, it does have some bright bedding plants, pleasant shrubs and summer flowering herbs, all well sheltered by thick yew hedges. One final point worthy of mention are the hollies in the eastern section of the park which can be found near Crown Gate East. These are attractive in winter with their large clusters of scarlet berries.

Victoria Park is spacious with much to do and a vital resource for the local population of Tower Hamlets. It is bounded on its south-western edge by Regent's Canal which provides you with a pleasant walk towards Mile End Underground Station.

THE WATERGARDENS
National Garden Scheme (NGS): see note on page 30

See illustration 10, between pages 32 and 33

Address: Warren Road, Kingston-on-Thames; **Owner**: Warren Road Residents' Association; **Location**: Half way up Kingston Hill, between Kingston Hill Rd and Coombe Lane; **Transport**: Norbiton train station; Bus 85,K6; **Opening Times**: NGS annual open day (see NGS book); **Seasonal Features**: Landscaped Japanese garden and spring blossom

The Watergardens in Kingston-on-Thames contains a well-maintained, nine acre Japanese water garden first established in 1865 as well as a rockery, a large pond and some impressive trees. Camellias, rhododendrons, azaleas, cherries, maples, cedars and beeches all abound and lead to much colour in spring and autumn. A lawn and flowerbed front the main house and run down to a peaceful pond containing an island of rhododendrons. From the bottom of the pond a stream runs out via a series of pools into the wooded area which contains the Japanese garden.

Enter the attractive, mossy woodland and you will find an intriguing garden with paths meandering round some old and unusual trees and shrubs and a good collection of primulas. A pergola stands partly concealed in rhododendrons and in the bottom rests a large pond criss-crossed by brightly coloured bridges. Leafy gunnera, weeping willows, ginkgos and maples all stand round the water's edge and a fountain plays in the sunlight breaking through the opening in the canopy overhead.

WATERLOW PARK
See illustration 28, between pages 96 and 97

Address: Highgate Hill, London N6; **Tel:** 020 7911 1693; **Owner**: Camden Council; **Location**: Next to Highgate Cemetery; **Transport**: Archway tube (Northern Line); Bus 143,210,271; **Entrance**: Free; **Opening Times**: Daily, 7.30am-dusk; **Other**

West Ham Park

Information:Aviary, cafe, children's playground, disabled access, dogs welcome, tennis courts; **Seasonal Features**: May, June, July, August, September, October; rhododendrons, herbaceous borders, autumnal trees, hollies.

Waterlow Park is a treat to visit. The land was donated to public usage in 1889 by the then Lord Mayor of London, Sir Sydney Waterlow, Bart., and a statue of him surveys a magnificent view of the City from the park's summit. Three lakes are joined by a stream and surrounded by weeping willows, maples, rhododendrons and swamp cypress trees. A hillside lawn supports a variety of spring flowers and a mixture of curious and ancient trees which, along with those in the old walled garden, help to form the jewel in the park's crown.

The trees in Waterlow Park are remarkable for their size, variety and seasonal colours. By the top lake there is a large weeping birch and a wishing tree with copper wishing tags tied on it. Old Lauderdale House at the top of the hill is a Grade II listed building dating from c1580. It is now used as a cafe and aromatic herbs are grown in raised beds outside. Two headless stone eagles guard the steps to the old walled garden, but pass between these and you find some magnificent trees including a huge ginkgo, a large tulip tree and a very elderly honey-locust tree (*Gleditsia tricanthos*). A variegated holly and giant copper beech give colour variation and two old magnolias by the entrance steps bear large white flowers in early summer. In winter a line of tall hollies along the far side of the walled garden add botanical interest.

In the spring the orchard and rhododendrons around the lakes are in bloom and wisteria, azaleas, irises and cherries all flower in the mixed herbaceous borders in the south of the park. Rich autumn colour is provided by chestnuts, oaks and maples. An avenue of mature limes passes through the centre of the park and a well-kept garden of shrubberies and mixed herbaceous beds lies down in the south east corner.

WEST HAM PARK

Address: Upton Lane, Forest Gate, London E7; **Tel**: 020 8472 3584; **Owner**: Corporation of London; **Transport**: Stratford tube (Central Line) and train station; Bus 104,238; **Entrance**: Free; **Opening Times**: Daily, 7.30am-sunset; **Other Information**: Children's playground, disabled access, dogs on leads only, events, sports facilities, talks held, toilets; **Seasonal Features**: March, April, May, June, July, August, September, October; heather bed, formal bedding, cherry blossom, irises, roses, autumnal trees, National Collection of *Trachelospermum* and *Liquidambar*, rock garden, Acer bed

West Ham Park is an oasis of green in the East End of London with character, colour and a choice of attractions throughout the year. It covers 77 acres of interesting parkland and garden which are well stocked with some good specimen trees and rare plants. The Corporation of London has two National Collections in the park – the *Liquidambar* genus known for attractive autumn foliage and the *Trachelospermum* genus which is cultivated for its fragrant flowers.

In 1762 the site was purchased by an eminent physician, botanist and patron of sciences, Dr John Fothergill. He set up a thriving 30 acre botanical garden there with a 67 metre long glasshouse and gathered over 3,400 plant species from all around the world. His collection rivalled that of Kew Gardens at the time. A ginkgo tree was planted in 1763 that still stands today and with plants retrieved from the Alps he laid out the Country's first purpose-built rock garden. This has recently been re-created. After Dr. Fothergill's death, the Park passed to the Gurney family and then to the Corporation of London.

There is still plenty of botanical interest left in West Ham Park. This is a well maintained park and a garden next to the main office contains bright Victorian-style bedding. A heather bed is in flower from February to April when a cherry avenue comes into bloom. In May iris and peony gardens blossom and later a nearby rose garden provides a riot of colour and scent with 70 different varieties. As well as the revered 240 year-old ginkgo tree the park contains many trees notable for their age or rarity. These include two uncommon *Quercus 'Fulhamensis'*, a magnificent weeping ash, a large oak-leafed hornbeam, a particularly old golden rain tree and an oak planted in 1887 to commemorate the Golden Jubilee of Queen Victoria. There are some fairly rare hollies which, together with the palm and snakebark maple by the New Zealand bed, give good winter interest.

Visitors will also encounter a lily pond, a children's playground, many sports facilities, a Victorian bandstand and a plant nursery. The nursery is one of the largest of its kind in London with over 200 plant species grown inside nine computer-controlled greenhouses. These produce about 300,000 bedding plants each year for the Corporation of London. Group tours of the nursery can be arranged via the park office.

West Ham Park is spacious, fun and vibrant with an interesting history that lives on today.

WESTMINSTER ABBEY GARDEN

Address:Westminster Abbey, London SW1P; **Tel**: 020 7654 4946; **Owner**:Westminster Abbey; **Location**:Westminster Abbey Cloisters, entrance from Dean's Yard; **Transport**: St James's Park & Westminster tubes (District & Circle Lines); Bus 11,24,88,211; **Entrance**: Free; **Opening Times**: Tues-Thurs 10am-6pm in summer, 10am-4pm in winter; **Other Information**: Abbey bookshop, disabled access, guide dogs only, refreshments; **Seasonal Features**: March, April, May; daffodils, cherry blossom

Two secret and historic gardens lie hidden deep within the walls of the complex of Westminster. Much the larger of the two is the 11th century College garden which measures slightly over one acre and rewards those who find it with a fine view of the Houses of Parliament and Westminster Abbey. It features a spacious main lawn with large clusters of spring flowers, well-matured London plane and cherry trees and some well-worn religious statues that seem very much at home within the 900 year old monastic garden.

In striking contrast to this sunny and relaxing setting with its stunning views is the second of the two gardens – the Little Cloister garden. This is an intriguing study in plant colour and texture complete with central fountain. The whole is planted in a small cloister which can be viewed from all sides. A visit to the gardens is especially recommended for a bright early spring day when the daffodils are in flower before leaves hide too much of the view.

Further Information

Other seasonal garden visiting opportunities in London:

Chelsea Flower Show – an exhibition of show gardens containing all that is considered new and fashionable in the horticultural world. Held at the end of May in the grounds of the Royal Hospital, Chelsea. For details, tel: 020 7649 1885

Hampton Court Palace Flower Show – an exhibition of majestic size of flowers, gardens and garden paraphernalia held in early July in the grounds of Hampton Court Palace. For details, tel: 020 7649 1885

London Garden Squares Day – an annual charity event organised by the London Historic Parks and Gardens Trust (LHPGT) and held on the first Sunday in June when over 40 private garden squares open to the public. Many are historic, secret and most beautifully maintained and details of participating squares can be obtained by sending a stamped addressed envelope to LHPGT, Duck Island Cottage, St James's Park, London SW1A 2BJ.

Day pass tickets to all the squares can be purchased either in advance from selected branches of Waterstones Bookshops Ltd or on the day from participating garden squares. The opening hours of participating squares are generally between 10am-5pm or 2-5pm and in some squares, music or teas will be provided. You should check each entry for a brief description and information on opening times, location, activities, the nearest bus and tube and wheelchair access.

The following squares are some of those you can visit on the day.

CLEVELAND SQUARE, W2: beautiful square with many large, old trees, a colourful herbaceous border and a small Japanese garden.

CONVENT OF THE ASSUMPTION GARDEN, W8: garden of the 140 year old convent containing a Lourdes type grotto with rabbits, goldfish and old fruit and plane trees.

DOVE GARDENS, SW7: a well kept secret garden restored in 1992 with the original Victorian planting where possible.

EDWARDES SQUARE, W8: large and attractive garden containing a croquet lawn, grass tennis court, children's playground and a small Greek temple. Paths meander through shrubberies and a rose pergola while trees tower overhead.

Museum of Garden History's regular lectures charting the inspirations, shapes and lasting influences of historic gardens and gardening. All events are held at The Ark, 220 Lambeth Road, London SE1 at which there is an attractive, paved garden. For further details contact the Reservations Secretary, Museum of Garden History, Lambeth Palace Road, London SE1 7LB; tel: 020 7401 8865; fax: 020 7401 8869.

Royal Horticultural Society's two-day seasonal Flower Shows at Westminster – featuring exhibits from Britain's top nurseries. There are several winter, spring, summer and autumn shows all held at the Royal Horticultural Society (RHS) Horticultural Halls in Vincent Square, London SW1 (nearest tube: Victoria or St James's Park). They reflect the changing seasons each year, progressing from early plants such as snowdrops and daffodils through to summer blooms and autumnal fruit and vegetables. The Spring Flower Show usually encompasses the London Orchid Show held in mid March. For details of annual shows and dates tel: 020 7649 1885, for tickets tel: 020 7316 4707.

Glossary

Arbour: A garden construction which shelters paths and seats and is often surrounded by plants.

Folly: An ornate building with a purely aesthetic function.

Gazebo: A building, usually in a raised position, from which the views are particularly good.

Grotto: An artificial underground cave made to feel both dank and mysterious.

Ha-ha: A large ditch separating a garden from fields beyond but unseen when viewed from the house.

Herbaceous Border: A flower bed of plants which die down in autumn and reappear the following spring.

Knot Garden: A geometrical pattern of beds of flowers, herbs or decorative gravel surrounded by close-trimmed box hedges. Popular in the 15th and 16th Centuries.

Old English Garden: A sheltered, walled garden with paths meandering past colourful, mixed, informal flower borders.

Order Bed: Flower bed in which plants which are closely related are found together.

Pagoda: Tall and decorative Buddhist tower of spiritual significance.

Parterre: An elaborate and intricately-designed garden often containing ornamental fountains, statues or urns. Fashionable at the end of the 17th century.

Pergola: A structure of posts, occasionally forming a tunnel, which is usually entwined with climbing plants.

Pleached Avenue: A tunnel or line of trees with their branches trained and intertwined horizontally.

Rotunda: A classical feature on a round plinth with a domed roof atop a circle of columns.

Topiary: Evergreen shrubs which have been clipped into ornamental shapes

Index

Illustrations are numbered 1–28. Numbers 1–13 are located between pages 32 and 33 and 14–28 between pages 96 and 97. Bold page references indicate main entries